IN THE HEAT OF THE KITCHEN

IN THE HEAT OF THE KITCHEN

GORDON RAMSAY

With Roz Denny and Mark Sargeant
Photographs by Georgia Glynn Smith

WILEY

John Wiley & Sons, Inc.

Dedication

For my youngest daughter, Matilda, born on my birthday.

Text Copyright © 2003, 2004 Gordon Ramsay

Photography Copyright © 2003 Georgia Glynn Smith

Design and layout Copyright © 2004 Quadrille Publishing Limited

First published in 2003 by Quadrille Publishing Limited, Alhambra House
27-31 Charing Cross Road, London WC2H 0LS

Published by John Wiley & Sons, Inc., Hoboken, New Jersey

For general information about our other products and services, please contact our
Customer Care Department within the United States at (800) 762-2974, outside
the United States at (317) 572-3993 or fax (317) 572-4002.

Wiley also publishes its books in a variety of electronic formats. Some content that
appears in print may not be available in electronic books. For more information about
Wiley products, visit our web site at www.wiley.com.

Library of Congress Cataloging-in-Publication Data:
ISBN 0 76458 834 6
Printed in China
10 9 8 7 6 5 4 3 2

NOTES

• *Recipes give both standard American measures and metric measures. The two sets of measurements are not exact equivalents, so use one or the other and not a combination.*

• *Egg sizes are specified in the recipes. I recommend eggs from cage-free birds. If you are pregnant or in a vulnerable health group, avoid those recipes that contain raw or lightly cooked eggs.*

• *Ovens should always be preheated to the specified temperature. Get to know your oven and use an oven thermometer to check its accuracy. My timings are provided as guidelines, with a description of color or texture where appropriate.*

INTRODUCTION

Food intrigued me from an early age. I wasn't brought up in a home where luxury food was the norm, far from it, but my mother was resourceful and we ate well. I also learned to value the freshness and quality of good ingredients first hand. Tasting the freshest salmon and sea trout, caught fishing with my father, was an early experience I will not forget. Fruit and vegetable picking, to supplement the family income, gave me the opportunity to appreciate homegrown foods, such as asparagus, peas, strawberries and raspberries, at their very best.

Food was a passion, but like most boys, I loved soccer and my ambition was to be a professional football player. I worked hard and achieved my goal, only to have my career cut short by injury. It was a huge disappointment, but it gave me the opportunity to explore my other great passion, and I trained as a chef. It was incredibly hard work, but I have no regrets. It is now over 15 years since I quit soccer and took up cooking. In that time I have learned an extraordinary amount about food, and life. I have learned from my own experiences, and from many others who have willingly passed on their knowledge and secrets to me. My first restaurant, Aubergine in London, put me on the culinary map and since then I have opened eight restaurants and I now employ hundreds of staff. Claridge's, The Connaught and The Savoy Grill in London are all Ramsay restaurants, and many of my staff have been with me since the start.

Along the way, I seem to have acquired the reputation of being something of a tyrant in the kitchen. I consider this a harsh judgement. My standards are high and I expect the same of my staff. It isn't a madly ambitious character or a competitive nature that drives me. It is simply my passion for great food, and my desire to share that with others. I try to ensure that I spend at least one service a day—lunch or dinner—in one of the kitchens. Consistent quality is vital and if anything isn't up to scratch, I need to get that across to my staff, as succinctly as possible. In the heat of the kitchen, when service is in full flow, there is little time for polite conversation.

When I am not in one of the kitchens, I am likely to be searching for inspiration for our menus. Food is constantly changing and that excites me. Whenever I can, I take off for a couple of days to visit a new region of France, Italy, or Spain, sample local specialties, and visit one or two restaurants a day. If a dish impresses me, I don't copy it, I break it down into its basic elements and reinvent. There are no gimmicks in my recipes. Paris always inspires and brings back memories of formative years, but I am increasingly impressed with the food of Barcelona, Spain, where Catalan-inspired dishes are achieving new heights. My venture to The States has opened up a whole new source of inspiration – fabulous quality ingredients and an amazing spectrum of cooking styles to experience. I am in my element.

Sometimes I'm asked what are the secrets of my success. The answers are simple—carefully sourced, high-quality ingredients, the skill and dedication of my chefs, and the techniques we use. So, in this book, I want to share with you some of the secrets that have helped me along the way. I have divided the chapters according to the type of food because many of the techniques that apply—to eggs, for example—relate to each other. Do take the time to read a recipe through carefully before you begin, to familiarize yourself with the method and any equipment you might need.

You do not need a battery of expensive tools to reproduce my recipes, but a good selection of sharpened knives is essential. At the very least you will need a large cook's knife, a small vegetable knife, a filleting knife, and a boning knife. Japanese knives impress me now, their stylish designs delivering accurate precision. Similarly, good, heavy, nonstick pans are vital. You cannot successfully pan-roast sweet, fresh scallops at a high heat in a flimsy, thin-based pan. We also use top-quality electric mixers and immersion blenders for our light mousses, sauces, and purées.

Finally, a few practical notes. Much of the fish and meat in this book is quickly cooked so it remains juicy and tender. This requires good-quality produce, so buy wisely from good suppliers. Likewise, some of the dishes use lightly cooked eggs and I suggest you buy eggs from cage-free birds, preferably organic. Measure carefully, ideally with a kitchen scale for accuracy. And remember that oven temperatures can only be guidelines, given that there is quite a variation between models. Check a dish a few minutes before it is supposed to come out of the oven and be prepared to allow longer if necessary. There is much more to good cooking than slavishly following instructions, even mine!

SHELLFISH

MOST CHEFS WILL TELL YOU *that the shellfish section in a restaurant kitchen is probably their favorite. I never cease to marvel at the wonderful creatures that land on our kitchen boards each day. In fact, we British chefs are quite spoiled. The cold waters around our coastline nurture fabulous, plump, sweet-fleshed lobsters, langoustines, and scallops. A popular dish on our Aubergine menu in the mid-1990s was sautéed scallops with crisp pan-fried potatoes and a fresh cream vinaigrette. One regular high-profile customer would make a special request for "no potatoes," in the hope we would fill the gaps on his plate with more sweet scallops. But I soon understood, and piled the salad leaves high instead.*

My earliest handling of shellfish was quite different. On the shores of Loch Lomond, in Scotland, my Dad, brother Ronnie, and I were in search of salmon and salmon trout. But first we needed bait. This came in the form of giant wild mussels and oysters, exposed as the tide went out. As an 11-year-old, I struggled to prise open large, obstinate oysters. I had no idea that a decade on I'd be relishing sipping the juice of oysters spiked with Tabasco and lemon.

Naturally, we buy shellfish in substantial quantities and only the best quality. I look to enhance the delicate flavors and textures of these creatures with simple poaching, steaming, or quick pan-frying. Of course, freshness is paramount. The best guarantee of absolute freshness is to buy your shellfish from a reputable

lobster, potato, and arugula salad

THIS SIMPLE, ELEGANT SALAD LOOKS STUNNING. *If you find that your lobster contains prized coral as you prepare it (look for a dark green sac), save it. This can be mixed into butter to dress fish steaks, or beaten and brushed on large raw shrimp prior to frying, to impart a superb flavor and vibrant orangey-pink color.* SERVES 2 AS A FIRST COURSE OR LIGHT DISH

2 small live lobsters, about 1 lb (500 g) each
4 teaspoons coarse sea salt
4 large boiling potatoes, about 4 oz (100 g) each
4 oz (100 g) arugula
½ cup (100 ml) Vinaigrette (page 218)
1-oz (25-g) piece Parmesan cheese
sea salt and freshly ground black pepper

First, put the lobsters in the freezer for about 30 minutes to make them sleepy. When ready to cook, make sure you kill them quickly: the simplest way is to detach the head from the body as fast and firmly as possible. Put the lobster, belly-side down, horizontally in front of you on a board. (The claws will be wrapped in thick bands so they won't nip you.) Hold the head firmly with one hand and, with your other hand, push the tail hard away from you, then toward you, in two swift moves. This detaches the head from the body quickly. (The two parts may continue to twitch a little because of cut nerve endings, but the lobster is no longer alive.)

Pull the large claws from the head and set aside. Discard the head (or use for lobster bisque, page 12). Clean the body by removing the swim bladder, which is attached to the middle tail section. Holding the body belly-side down, fan out the tail and grasp the middle tail section between your finger and thumb. Bend it upward, then twist and gently pull to remove the long, thin, opaque tube. Repeat to prepare the other lobster. Tie the tail sections together to obtain perfect medallions (see right).

Put a large pan containing at least 3 quarts (3 liters) of water on to boil and add the salt. Drop in the lobster bodies and claws and boil, allowing 3½ minutes for the tails, up to 5 minutes for the claws. Remove and cool a little. Pull the shells from the bodies—it is best to do this while they are still warm. Crack the claws with the back of a heavy cook's knife. Then you should be able to pull off the shell in two parts and extract the meat in one piece; set aside.

Meanwhile, boil the potatoes in salted water until just tender. Remove and cool a little, then peel them while still warm (wearing rubber gloves to protect your hands from the heat).

Blitz half the arugula in a food processor with a little of the vinaigrette, then drizzle in the rest until the dressing is velvety smooth. Taste for seasoning.

Slice the potatoes lengthwise and arrange in the center of each serving plate. Spoon some of the dressing over them. Cut the lobster tails into medallions and arrange on top. Add the claw meat, if desired. Drizzle with more dressing and add the remaining arugula leaves. Using a swivel peeler, pare fine shavings of Parmesan and scatter over the arugula leaves. Serve at once.

PERFECT MEDALLIONS

To obtain neat, round medallions, uncurl the lobster tails and press them together, flesh sides inward, placing them head to tail as shown. Tie securely along the length with kitchen string to ensure the lobster tails remain straight as they cook.

lobster bisque

THIS GOURMET SOUP IS LIGHT AND DELICATE *with an intense shellfish flavor. There's nothing difficult about it, you simply use the heads and shells of lobsters rather than throw them away. Of course, lobster carcasses can be kept in the freezer until you want to make the bisque. Langoustine and crab shells are suitable, too. You'll need a heavy-bladed knife or a Chinese chopper to cut up the shells.* SERVES 2–3 AS A FIRST COURSE

shells and heads of 2 lobsters

6 tablespoons olive oil

1 medium onion, minced

2 carrots, minced

1 celery stalk or ½ fennel bulb,
    chopped

1 fat garlic clove, chopped

2 lemon grass stems, chopped

generous pinch of saffron strands
    (optional)

2 teaspoons Cognac

7 fl oz (200 ml) Noilly Prat or other
    dry vermouth

4 cups (1 liter) Fish Stock (page 209)

3 plum tomatoes, chopped

1 tablespoon tomato paste

1 large sprig each of basil, tarragon,
    and parsley

1 bay leaf

½ cup (100 ml) heavy cream

generous pinch of cayenne pepper

sea salt and freshly ground black pepper

Chop up the lobster shells and heads, using a large, heavy knife or Chinese cleaver—the finer you chop them, the more flavor you will extract. Retain the soft tissue in the heads—this adds to the flavor.

Heat half the olive oil in a large saucepan and sauté the lobster shells and heads for about 5 minutes. Remove them with a slotted spoon and set aside.

Heat the remaining oil in the pan, then add the vegetables, garlic, and lemon grass. Sauté for about 5 minutes until softened. Sprinkle in the saffron, if using, and cook for 30 seconds.

Deglaze with the Cognac, then add the Noilly Prat and bubble until reduced by half. Return the shells to the pan. Add the stock, tomatoes, tomato paste, and herbs. Season with pepper to taste (salt won't be necessary). Bring to a boil, then lower the heat and simmer for 20 minutes.

Strain the liquid through a large sieve into another pan, pressing the shells with the back of a ladle to extract as much flavor as possible.

Bring the strained liquid to a boil and simmer until reduced to about 2 cups (500 ml). Stir in the cream and bring to a gentle simmer. Cook gently for 4 to 5 minutes. Check the seasoning, adding salt to taste at this stage and cautious pinches of cayenne. Serve hot.

CHEF'S SECRET *Noilly Prat is one of my secret flavorings. This classic vermouth, with its hint of sweet aniseed, is perfect for enhancing fish and shellfish. I often use it in combination with a little Cognac. Like sherry, it is a fortified wine, so once opened it can be kept in the pantry.*

smoked haddock and clam chowder

THERE IS SOME CONTROVERSY *as to whether chowder should have a cream base in the manner of the New Englanders, or a tomato base—the Manhattan alternative. Personally, I prefer the cream base I've used in this recipe. The light smokiness of the haddock and the sublime velvety texture of this chowder make it outrageously good.* SERVES 4 AS A FIRST COURSE OR LIGHT DISH

Wash the clams thoroughly, discarding any that are open and refuse to close when sharply tapped.

Pour the milk into a large saucepan or sauté pan and bring to a boil. Reduce the heat to a simmer and add the haddock fillet. Poach gently for 3 to 4 minutes until the fish is just starting to flake. Carefully lift the haddock out of the milk on to a plate and set aside to cool. Flake the fish into bite-sized pieces, checking to make sure all small bones have been removed.

Put the wine into a large pan (which has a tight-fitting lid) and bring to a boil over medium-high heat. Add the clams, cover, and cook for 2 to 3 minutes until the shells open. Immediately remove from the heat and drain, reserving the cooking broth. Discard any unopened clams.

Strain the reserved cooking broth through a strainer lined with cheesecloth. Shuck the clams and set aside.

Heat the olive oil in a medium pan, add the shallot and sweat for 2 to 3 minutes until translucent but not colored (see below). Add the potatoes and cook for 2 minutes, again not allowing them to color.

Add the reserved broth from the clams and simmer until the liquid has reduced by half. Add the fish stock and cream and continue to simmer for a further 15 minutes.

Remove from the heat and purée the mixture, using a hand-held stick blender, or in a blender or food processor. Pour the mixture through a fine sieve or mouli into a clean pan, then add the mustard and season with salt and pepper to taste.

Reserve 4 clams and some flakes of smoked haddock for garnish. Add the rest to the soup and reheat gently, but do not allow to boil.

Divide the chowder among four warmed serving bowls and garnish with the reserved haddock flakes and clams.

1 lb (500 g) clams in the shell
2 cups (500 ml) milk
1 fillet smoked haddock, about 1 lb (500 g)
½ cup (125 ml) dry white wine
2 tablespoons olive oil
1 large shallot, finely sliced
2 large potatoes (preferably waxy), peeled and thinly sliced
2 cups (500 ml) Fish Stock (page 209)
4 cups (1 liter) heavy cream
1 tablespoon wholegrain mustard
sea salt and freshly ground black pepper

SWEATING VEGETABLES *We use the term "sweat" to describe gently cooking sliced or diced vegetables in oil over medium-low heat to enhance their natural sweetness and flavor. The aim is to soften the vegetables without allowing them to color, which would spoil the finished result.*

herb brioche crusted mussels

THESE MAKE A GOOD PARTY CANAPÉ, *or first course, and you can assemble them an hour or two ahead. Cooked mussels in their half-shell are topped with moist, herby brioche crumbs and gratinéed under the broiler. I always use freshly cooked mussels, but you do need large ones. If you can only find small fresh mussels, buy about 20 of the New Zealand green-lipped variety instead—these are sold ready cooked in the half-shell. If sweet brioche from a bakery is the only option for the crumb topping, substitute a rich bread, such as foccacia.* SERVES 4 AS A FIRST COURSE

2¼ lb (1 kg) large, fresh mussels
1 shallot, sliced
¾ cup white wine
1 tablespoon (15 g) butter
sea salt and freshly ground black pepper

Topping:
3–4 tablespoons olive oil
1 shallot, minced
4 cups (200 g) fine crumbs of unsweetened brioche,
    without crusts
1 thyme sprig, leaves only, minced
2–3 cilantro sprigs, minced
1 teaspoon minced chives
3½ tablespoons (20 g) freshly grated Parmesan cheese

TO CLEAN MUSSELS *Mussels that you buy are cultivated in protected areas of the sea bed, or grown on poles fixed in clean sea water. Because of their habitat, they ingest sand and grit as they feed. Live mussels must be bought very fresh. Scrub them clean and remove any barnacles under cold water, using a stiff brush. Then, if time, put the mussels in a large bowl of clean, cold, salted water, sprinkle in a handful of oats, and set aside for a few hours. The mussels will feed on the oats and expel any grit they contain.*

Wash the mussels thoroughly, pull away any beards, and scrub the shells to remove any barnacles. Discard any mussels that are open and refuse to close when you tap them sharply.

Heat a large saucepan until hot, then tip in the mussels, sliced shallot, wine, butter, and seasoning. Cover with a tight-fitting lid and cook for about 5 minutes, shaking the pan occasionally. By this time the mussels should have opened; discard any that are still closed.

Drain the mussels and leave until cool enough to handle. Remove the mussels from their shells, reserving 20 to 30 of the largest half-shells.

Meanwhile, make the topping. Heat 1 tablespoon olive oil in a small pan and sauté the shallot for about 3 minutes until softened, without coloring. Add to the brioche crumbs along with the minced herbs and Parmesan. Mix with a fork, adding more oil to moisten as necessary; the crumb mixture should not be dry.

Put 2 or 3 mussels in each of the reserved half-shells. Sprinkle the crumb topping over the mussels to cover them completely and press down lightly.

When ready to serve, preheat a foil-lined baking pan under the broiler. Lay the mussels in the pan and broil, close to the heat, for a few minutes, until the topping is lightly browned and the mussels are piping hot.

GREEN-LIPPED MUSSELS *Use these if you cannot find large, fresh mussels. To prepare, wipe the mussels clean. Put them, in their half-shells, on a baking sheet in a preheated oven at 350°F (180°C) for 5 minutes to warm through. Top with the crumb mixture and gratiné under the broiler as described.*

marinated oyster and fennel salad

IF THE NOTION OF EATING RAW OYSTERS *from the shell doesn't appeal to you, then try them marinated—the best of both worlds. For this salad, shucked oysters are marinated in citrus juices with soy and sesame flavorings, then served on a crisp fennel salad. To serve 4, buy twice as many oysters, but you'll only need to increase the marinade by half as much again. Use a mandoline or Japanese slicer to slice the fennel.* SERVES 2 AS A FIRST COURSE OR LIGHT LUNCH

12 freshly shucked Pacific or flat oysters
   (see below), juices reserved
1 large fennel bulb
about 4 oz (100 g) curly endive
   or arugula
1 tablespoon chopped chives
3 tablespoons Vinaigrette (page 218)
sea salt and freshly ground black pepper

Marinade:
1 large shallot, minced
juice of 2 limes
juice of ½ lemon
1 tablespoon dark soy sauce
1 tablespoon toasted sesame oil
few drops of Tabasco sauce
sea salt and freshly ground black pepper

Check over the shucked oysters carefully, removing any tiny fragments of shell. Wash them carefully in their reserved juices, then chill.

Remove the fronds from the fennel and reserve for garnish. With the tip of a very sharp, small knife, cut out the core from the base of the fennel and discard. Fill a large bowl with cold water and tip in three or four handfuls of ice cubes. Peel away the outside ribs of the fennel bulb, using a swivel vegetable peeler.

Slice the fennel very finely from the cored end using a mandoline, then drop straight into the ice water. Leave the fennel in the ice water for an hour or so; this helps it to become very crisp.

In the meantime, mix the marinade ingredients together in a shallow dish. Add the oysters and toss to mix. Let marinate for about 15 minutes.

Drain the fennel and pat dry with a clean towel. To serve, toss the crisp fennel with the endive or arugula, chives, vinaigrette, and seasoning. Divide between plates. Using a slotted spoon or fork, lift the oysters from the marinade and arrange them around the salad. Trickle a little marinade over them and garnish with fennel fronds.

TO SHUCK OYSTERS *The two main species of oyster available are smooth-shelled flat oysters (or belons) and the more craggy Pacific oysters, which are easier to open. The classic short, stubby oyster knife is the safest implement to use. Make sure the oyster shells are tightly closed; discard any that are not. Take the knife in one hand and protect your other hand with a thick, folded napkin or towel. Hold the oyster rounded side down in the cloth or towel with the hinge end showing. Keeping the oyster level, slowly but firmly stick the knife point in through the hinge, wiggling it from side to side if necessary, until you feel a "give" as the hinge muscle is cut. Insert the knife a bit farther and twist to lift up the top shell. Tip out the juices into a bowl. Slide the knife under the oyster to cut through the muscle and take out the oyster. Check that it is free of small pieces of shell. Rinse the oysters in their own juices, then chill.*

pan-fried soft-shell crabs with lemon and capers

I AM AN AVID FAN OF THE AMERICAN BLUE CRAB—*both in its hard- or soft-shell state. The best soft-shelled crabs come from Chesapeake. Fry the soft-shell crabs in plenty of unsalted butter and you can literally eat these delicacies straight out of the pan. While they need little extra adornment, I love them with a simple caper and lemon sauce. Use two large skillets so that you can cook and serve all eight crabs at the same time.* SERVES 4 AS A FIRST COURSE OR LIGHT LUNCH

Dredge the crabs in the flour to coat evenly, shaking off excess.

Heat two 12-inch (30 cm) skillets over high heat until you can feel the heat rising from the pan. Add 4 tablespoons of butter to each pan. Swirl the pans as the butter melts to prevent it from burning.

When the foaming subsides add the crabs, shell-side down, placing four in each pan, and seal over high heat for 30 seconds on each side. Lower the heat to prevent the crabs from burning and pan-fry for 2 minutes until they turn reddish brown in color. Using tongs, turn the crabs over and cook for a further 1 to 2 minutes on the other side.

Immediately transfer the crabs to serving plates. Pour off the butter from one of the pans, then melt the remaining butter in this pan. Quickly add the lemon juice, sherry vinegar, capers, scallion, chopped herbs, and seasoning. Bring to a boil and then pour over the crabs. Serve immediately.

8 soft-shell crabs

2 cups (250 g) all-purpose flour

10 tablespoons unsalted butter

3 tablespoons lemon juice

2 teaspoons sherry vinegar

2 teaspoons chopped capers

1 medium scallion, trimmed and finely chopped

2 teaspoons chopped tarragon

2 tablespoons chopped parsley

sea salt and freshly ground black pepper

CHEF'S SECRET *American blue crabs are harvested just as they are about to grow and lose their shells, when they are succulent and full of flavor. Make sure you seal them over high heat to retain all the delicious juices and flavors of the sea.*

CHEF'S SECRET *We never discard anything that can be used to impart flavor, and that includes scallop corals. The fresh corals are spread on a sheet of parchment paper and dried overnight in a very low oven until they are hard and brittle, then blitzed in a food processor, or ground to a powder. We sprinkle this coral powder over fish dishes, risottos, and creamy sauces for pasta. It lends a superb flavor.*

truffle-dressed scallop salad

SCALLOPS TASTE WONDERFUL *and can be served in a variety of ways, though they are quite expensive. I use only hand-dived king scallops from Scotland, which are delivered so fresh they almost pulsate when we prise them open. After cleaning, we wash and dry the scallops, then stack them upright in lines in containers and chill overnight to firm up. Sea scallops are very meaty, so you don't need many per person.* SERVES 4 AS A FIRST COURSE OR LIGHT MEAL

Hold the scallop rounded-side down in the palm of your hand and stick the tip of a sharp, strong knife in between the two shells, close to the hinge. Work the knife along the hinge to sever the muscle that holds the shells together. Lift off the top shell, then slip your knife under the nugget of meat with its orange coral and frilly skirt, to ease it away from the shell. Pull away the skirt and remove the black intestinal thread and muscle at the side. Separate the coral from the nugget; wash and dry, then cut each scallop in half horizontally. Chill until ready to cook.

Wash and dry the salad leaves, tear into pieces, and toss together in a bowl.

To make the dressing, put the egg yolk, sherry vinegar, mustard, and seasoning into a small mixing bowl and set on a damp cloth to hold it steady. Mix the peanut and olive oils together in a small cup, then gradually whisk into the egg yolk base, a few drops at a time. Keep whisking briskly, and make sure each tiny addition of oil is emulsified before adding more. As the dressing starts to thicken, you can slowly trickle in the oil, whisking all the time. When it is thick, whisk in the truffle oil. Check the seasoning and set aside.

Par-boil the potatoes for 5 minutes, then drain and peel while still warm. Let cool, then cut into slices about ½ inch (1 cm) thick. Heat 3 tablespoons olive oil in a frying pan and sauté the potato slices, in batches as necessary. Fry in a single layer in the pan for 2 to 3 minutes on each side until brown and crisp on the outside and cooked through. Keep warm.

Dust the scallops lightly with curry powder and seasoning. Heat a heavy-based frying pan or ridged grill pan until very hot. Add a thin film of oil, then place the scallops in the pan, in a circle. Cook for 1 minute, then turn (in the same order you put them in the pan, to ensure even cooking). Cook the other side for 30 to 60 seconds, until golden. Remove from the pan; let rest for 2 to 3 minutes.

Meanwhile, toss the salad leaves in a little vinaigrette and season. Cut the truffle, if using, into wafer-thin slices. Arrange the potato slices, scallops, and truffle slices in a circle on each serving plate. Place a tall cutter in the center and fill with the salad leaves, then carefully lift it off to leave an impressive tower of salad leaves. (Alternatively, you can simply pile the leaves into the center.) Beat 3 to 4 tablespoons of hot water into the truffle dressing to loosen it, then spoon around the salad. Drizzle any remaining dressing over the top and serve.

6–10 sea scallops

7 oz (200 g) mixed salad leaves (such as curly endive, arugula, oak leaf lettuce)

8 large boiling potatoes, about 4 oz (100 g) each

olive oil, for frying

a little curry powder, for dusting

a little Vinaigrette (page 218)

½ fresh truffle (optional)

sea salt and freshly ground black pepper

Truffle dressing:

1 extra large egg yolk

1 teaspoon sherry vinegar

½ teaspoon English mustard powder

large pinch of fine sea salt

pinch of freshly ground white pepper

4½ tablespoons peanut oil

5½ tablespoons olive oil

1 teaspoon truffle-scented oil

langoustine cocktail

THIS IS MY ULTIMATE SHRIMP COCKTAIL! *Rather than use shrimp, I buy fresh langoustines (also called lobsterettes, Dublin Bay prawns, or scampi). These coldwater crustaceans are not cheap, but they have the most wonderful sweet flavor. Our supplies are from western Scotland. I poach the langoustines gently in a vegetable nage, then serve them simply with a mayonnaise-based sauce on a shredded romaine salad. You can also use raw tiger shrimp.* SERVES 4 AS A FIRST COURSE

20 fresh langoustines (lobsterettes)
2 cups (500 ml) Vegetable Nage (page 211)

Sauce:
½ cup (100 ml) Mayonnaise (page 219)
2 teaspoons ketchup
1 teaspoon Worcestershire sauce
1 tablespoon Cognac
few drops of Tabasco

Salad:
1 romaine heart
1 tablespoon minced shallot
1 tablespoon diced crisp, sharp apple (Granny Smith)
few basil leaves, finely shredded
1–2 tablespoons Vinaigrette (page 218)
sea salt and freshly ground black pepper

For serving:
pinch of mild curry powder
1 cherry tomato, quartered
½ lemon, peeled and segmented
4 parsley sprigs

Bring a large pan of water to a boil. Drop in half of the langoustines and blanch for 30 seconds, then immediately drain and peel (see below). Devein by removing the black intestinal line that runs along the back of each one. Repeat with the remaining langoustines.

Bring the vegetable nage to a boil in a pan, then lower the heat to a simmer. Drop in the langoustines and poach for 2 to 3 minutes. Remove the pan from the heat and let the shellfish cool in the liquid.

Meanwhile, make the sauce: Put the mayonnaise in a bowl and mix in the ketchup, Worcestershire sauce, Cognac, and Tabasco to taste.

For the salad, roll up the romaine leaves and shred fairly finely. Put in a bowl with the shallot, apple, basil, and vinaigrette, and toss to mix. Season to taste.

When ready to serve, remove the langoustines from the nage with a slotted spoon and season lightly. Put a spoonful of sauce in the bottom of each of four cocktail glasses and scatter the salad on top. Arrange the langoustines on the salad. Trickle a little sauce over the top and dust very lightly with curry powder. Garnish each cocktail with a cherry tomato quarter, one or two lemon segments, and a parsley sprig. Serve at once.

HANDLING LANGOUSTINES *We buy our langoustines still alive. They are aggressive creatures and attack each other, so top quality langoustines are often sold in individual tubes to keep them apart. To make them easier to peel, we first blanch the langoustines in boiling water, about ten at a time, for 30 seconds, to loosen the shells. As they are easier to shell while still hot, we peel the langoustines as soon as we can handle them. Pull the head from the body, so the tail meat remains intact, then crack the top of the tail shell with the back of a knife. Push up the meat from the tail end and it should pop out perfectly peeled and in one piece. Save the heads, shells, and legs—these are full of flavor and make excellent stock to use for fish soups and sauces. You can always freeze them and make the stock at a later date.*

CHEF'S SECRET *To check that the crab meat is free from shell, flake it over a metal tray. If there are any shell fragments, you will hear the sound as they fall on the metal.*

dressed crab with sauce gribiche

FOR OPTIMUM FLAVOR, *if possible buy live crabs. Otherwise I recommend that you buy freshly cooked crabs from your fishmonger or supermarket fresh fish counter and prepare them yourself (following the illustrated technique on the next page). European crabs have both white meat and creamy brown meat, and I prefer to flavor the two types of meat before spooning it back into the shells. Serve with toasted country-style bread.* SERVES 4 AS A FIRST COURSE, OR 2 AS A LIGHT MAIN COURSE

2 fresh crabs, each about 1–1¼ lb
  (500–600 g)
2½ cups (110 g) fine, fresh
  bread crumbs
squeeze of lemon juice
few drops of Tabasco
few drops of Worcestershire sauce
1–2 tablespoons Mayonnaise
  (page 219)
1 teaspoon each chopped parsley
  and cilantro
sea salt and freshly ground black pepper

Sauce:
3 hard-boiled large eggs, roughly
  chopped
1 large egg yolk
1 teaspoon Dijon mustard
½ teaspoon anchovy paste
1¼ cups (300 ml) sunflower or light
  olive oil
1 tablespoon white wine vinegar
1 teaspoon minced capers
1 teaspoon minced gherkins
1 teaspoon each chopped parsley,
  chervil, and tarragon

For serving:
1 large egg, hard-boiled and halved
2 teaspoons drained, chopped capers
2 teaspoons minced gherkin
1 tablespoon chopped parsley

If using live crabs, check the claws are well secured with strong bands. Then lay each crab on its back and, using an awl (or small ice pick), pierce the main nerve center point behind the eyes repeatedly (from different angles) to kill it. Plunge the crabs into a large pan of boiling water or Court Bouillon (page 208) and boil, allowing about 10 minutes; do not overcook. Remove and cool, then chill (this "sets" the meat and makes it easier to extract).

Meanwhile, make the sauce: Rub the hard-boiled eggs through a sieve into a bowl using the back of a ladle; set aside. Mix the raw egg yolk with the mustard, anchovy paste, and some seasoning in a bowl. Gradually whisk in the oil, drop by drop to begin with, then in a steady stream (as if you were making a mayonnaise). Stir in all of the remaining ingredients, including the sieved egg. Check the seasoning, then cover and chill until ready to serve.

Prepare the fresh crabs and extract the meat, keeping the white and brown meat separate (as described on the next page). To prepare the empty shells for serving, remove the thin undershell by cutting along the natural line, using pincers or pliers. Wash the shell thoroughly and dry well.

Put the brown meat into a blender with the bread crumbs, lemon juice, Tabasco, and Worcestershire sauce, and whiz very briefly to mix. Season with salt and pepper. (If you have no brown meat in your crab, use about one-fourth of the white meat to make this mixture.)

Flake the white meat and add the 1 to 2 tablespoons of mayonnaise, the parsley, cilantro, and seasoning. Toss with a fork to mix.

To serve, rub the egg yolk and white through a sieve with the back of a ladle, keeping them separate. Mix the chopped capers and gherkin together.

Spoon the brown crab meat into both sides of the cleaned crab shell, then spoon the white meat into the center, piling it up well. Garnish with lines of chopped parsley and sieved egg white and yolk (as shown). Put a spoonful of the caper and gherkin mixture on each portion of brown meat. Serve with the sauce.

PREPARING A FRESH CRAB

The crab shown here is a European brown crab.
Other crabs can be prepared in the same way.
Lay the crab on its back on a clean surface and twist
off the large claws.
Hold the shell firmly and push the body section up
with your thumbs—it should come out in one piece.
Remove the small stomach sac behind the mouth.
Pull away the inedible, feathery gray gills ("dead
man's fingers") from the body section and discard.
Twist off the legs.
Now, if there is any creamy brown meat in the main
shell, loosen it with a teaspoon—you should then be
able to tip it out easily into a bowl.
Break the large claws with one sharp knock from a
mallet and peel away the shell, then ease out the meat
in one piece with your thumbs.
Prise out the white meat from the body section and legs,
using a pick or skewer.
Keep the firm white meat and soft brown meat
separate, and check for any stray fragments of shell.

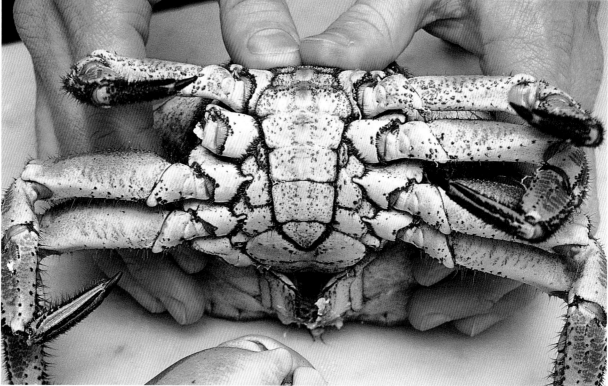

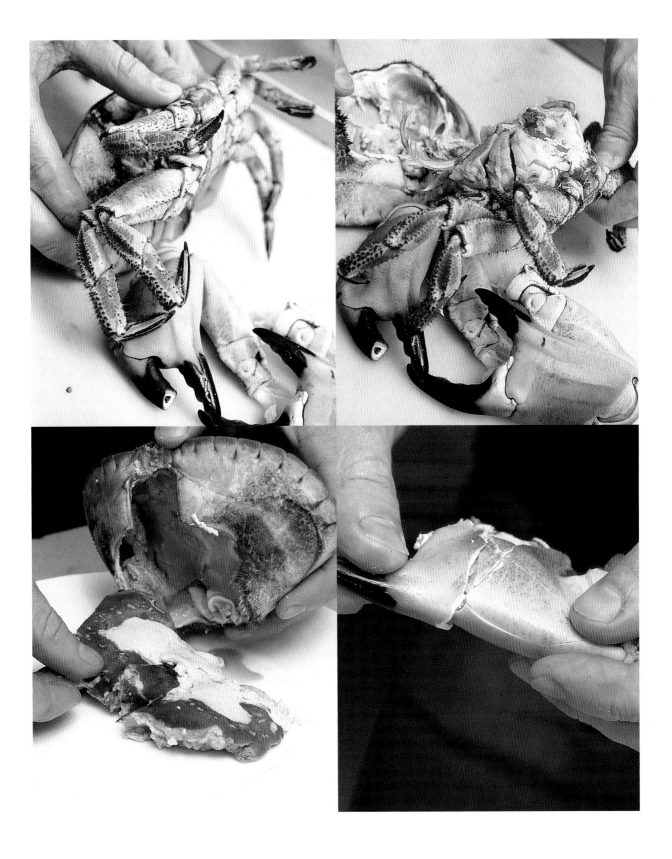

FISH

THE FISH SECTION WAS THE FIRST *I ran as Chef de partie in London's Le Gavroche. It was perhaps the busiest section because fish featured as first and main courses. Lackey, the fishmonger, delivered the early morning's catch from Brixham around 3:30 each afternoon. The delivery coincided with the end of lunch service and it had to be dealt with pretty quickly. There was little time for a break before starting evening service—all that filleting, trimming, and skinning, not to mention handling the wriggling langoustines.*

Lackey still delivers to me each day, his blue eyes flashing "It's up to you now," as he hands over the most perfect specimens you'll ever see. Few chefs survived the fish section without some scars—"Death Row," we used to call it. But the selection of fish supplied to Le Gavroche was the best I'd ever seen—small whole turbot, scaly sturgeon, zander, glistening mullets, and a terrific variety of fish for the best bouillabaisse and bourride served in town.

Fish continues to give me the opportunity to reinvent classic dishes in a contemporary way. Simplicity is the essence. Thick, juicy cod fillets are steamed with spices, garlic, and fresh herbs; broiled or fried fish are served simply with a red pepper mayonnaise; while terre et mer dishes, such as monkfish wrapped in bacon, combine flavors of the land and sea. Mackerel still remains one of my favorites—juicy and meaty with an almost earthy flavor, to team with full-flavored garlic, spices, sharp vinegars, and fruits. If we eat more mackerel, our cod stocks might have the chance to revive ...

mackerel and confit potato cups

FRESH MACKEREL IS AN UNDERRATED FISH, *which is a great shame because it has a good flavor and an excellent texture, and it's not expensive. Of course, you need to choose mackerel that is very fresh and firm.* SERVES 6 AS A FIRST COURSE

1 large eggplant

olive oil, for drizzling

2 large boiling potatoes, about 10 oz
   (300 g in total)

½ lb (250 g) butter, diced

6 large mackerel fillets, about 5 oz
   (150 g) each

juice of 1 lemon

1 tablespoon chopped cilantro

1 tablespoon chopped basil

sea salt and freshly ground black pepper

Tapenade:

2-oz (50-g) can anchovy fillets, drained

1⅓ cups (200 g) pitted black olives

2 tablespoons drained capers

1 fat garlic clove, crushed

1 tablespoon extra virgin olive oil

Slice the eggplant lengthwise as thinly as possible—a mandoline or Japanese slicer is the best implement to use. Discard the end pieces. Preheat a ridged grill pan until very hot. Cook the eggplant slices on the grill pan, in batches, for 2 to 3 minutes, turning to color both sides. Transfer to a shallow dish and drizzle lightly with olive oil, then brush to coat all over. Set aside to cool.

Peel the potatoes, then cut into slices ½ inch (1 cm) thick. Melt the butter in a shallow pan over low heat and heat slowly for 2 to 3 minutes to 212°F (100°C). Add the potato slices in an even layer and cook gently for about 12 minutes until softened. Remove the potato slices from the butter and drain on paper towels.

Meanwhile, heat the broiler. Place the mackerel skin-side down on the broiler rack and brush with a little olive oil. Season with salt and pepper, and trickle on the lemon juice. Broil, 4 inches (10 cm) from the heat, for 5 to 7 minutes until the flesh feels firm. Let cool, then remove the skin and divide the fish into flakes.

Now assemble the molds: Line two large teacups or similar shaped 7-oz (200-ml) molds with plastic wrap. Line the molds with the eggplant slices, overlapping slightly and bringing the slices up over the sides (to allow sufficient overhang to cover the top). Cover the bottom with a layer of potato slices, press down lightly, season, and sprinkle with the herbs. Next, press a layer of mackerel flakes on top. Repeat these layers twice, then top with a final layer of potato.

Fold the overhanging eggplant slices over to cover the top and press down lightly. Place on a small tray, cover with a board, weight down with cans of food, and refrigerate for a few hours, or preferably overnight.

Shortly before serving, whiz the tapenade ingredients in a food processor until smooth. Unmold the eggplant cups, remove the plastic wrap, and place on a board. Cut into slices and serve with the tapenade and coarse sea salt.

INDIVIDUAL TIMBALES
Individual-sized cups look equally stunning. Use tiny ramekins or similar molds—no more than 7 or 8 tablespoons (100 ml) capacity as the dish is quite rich.

CHEF'S SECRET *Caramelized eggplant slices give these attractive cups a unique flavor. To intensify their flavor, the wafer-thin eggplant slices are cooked dry (without oil) on a grill pan over a high heat until charred and caramelized, then drizzled with olive oil and left to cool. The oil imparts flavor and helps to soften the eggplants as they cool. Alternatively, you can create a similar effect by broiling the eggplant slices dry, then using a red-hot skewer to mark scorch lines before drizzling with oil.*

snapper baked in a salt crust

THIS CLEVER MEDITERRANEAN TECHNIQUE *overcomes the problem of dryness so often associated with oven-baked fish. The whole fish is encased in salt, which protects it from the intense heat of the oven, seals in the juices, and crisps the skin. The result is superb, succulent fish that, surprisingly, doesn't taste salty. Serve the baked red snapper with lemon wedges and a garlicky mayonnaise.*
SERVES 2–3 AS A MAIN DISH

1 red snapper, about 1¾–2¼ lb
    (800 g–1 kg), with head, fins, tail,
    and scales intact
5 cups (750 g) coarse sea salt
handful of thyme or rosemary sprigs

For serving:
parsley sprigs
lemon wedges
Garlic Mayonnaise (page 219)

Preheat the oven to 425°F (220°C). Rinse the fish and shake to remove excess water, but leave the skin moist.

Lay a large sheet of foil in a shallow roasting pan. Spread half the salt on the foil to make a bed, scatter on half of the herb sprigs, and place the fish on top. Scatter the remaining herb sprigs over the fish, then pour on the remaining salt to cover the fish. Press the salt up against the sides of the fish, then scrunch up the edges of the foil to hold it in place. Don't seal the foil over the top, as steam must be allowed to escape if the skin is to crisp.

Bake for 20 minutes, then remove from the oven and let stand for 10 minutes. Break off the crisp salt layer, then slide a long metal spatula underneath the fish and carefully lift it onto a board.

Peel off the skin, which will be easy to remove, and fillet the fish neatly to the bone. Remove the whole skeleton and fillet the fish underneath. The flesh will be moist and juicy. Carefully transfer the filleted fish to a serving platter and garnish with parsley. Serve with lemon wedges and garlic mayonnaise.

BAKING FISH IN A SALT CRUST *This is an excellent way to oven-cook whole fish, such as snapper or sea bream. You need a fish with scales intact, and one that has been gutted neatly so the opening can be pinched together to prevent salt from seeping inside. The salt forms a brittle coating that is easily broken away after baking, to reveal a perfectly cooked fish.*

broiled snapper with lemon grass and thyme velouté

SNAPPER IS A GLAMOROUS FISH, *its silky red coat giving it a distinctive appearance, with a flavor to match. Nothing could be more seductive than broiling it until the skin is crisp and the flesh succulent. I like to serve it with a velouté delicately scented with thyme and lemon grass, so the fish takes center stage.* SERVES 4 AS A MAIN DISH

Make the velouté and set aside.

Preheat the broiler. Brush the fish fillets with a little olive oil and place skin-side up on a baking tray.

Place under the broiler and cook for about 3 minutes until the skin is crispy. Turn and cook for a further 30 seconds. Remove from the heat and let rest for a few minutes, then season with salt and pepper to taste.

Reheat the velouté gently, if necessary. Pour a little sauce onto the center of each warmed plate and place the broiled snapper fillets, skin-side up, on top. Scatter with a few thyme sprigs and serve immediately.

2 cups (500 ml) Thyme and Lemon Grass Velouté (page 212), made with fish stock

4 red snapper fillets, about 6 oz (175 g) each

olive oil, for brushing

sea salt and freshly ground black pepper

thyme sprigs, to garnish

BROILING FISH FILLETS *To protect the flesh and give the skin a crisp texture and inviting color, most of the cooking should be on the skin side. To check it is cooked, press the flesh with the back of a fork. It should feel just firm with a very slight "give." Always season fish after cooking.*

CHEF'S SECRET

To impart a delicate flavor, drizzle a little olive oil onto the red mullet skin, then sprinkle with saffron strands and rub with your fingertips. Let infuse for 5 minutes or so. You'll find the saffron flavor permeates the fish and the skin cooks to a deep golden-red color.

warm red mullet salad

WITH ITS PROVENÇAL FLAVORS, *this eye-catching dish makes an inviting first course or chic light meal. Red mullet are increasingly on sale here. Buy whole fish and fillet them yourself (following the instructions below), or ask your fishmonger or fresh fish counter to do it for you. I like to enhance the attractive red-pink color of the mullet skins with saffron (see below).*
SERVES 4 AS A FIRST COURSE OR LIGHT MEAL

Check the red mullet fillets carefully with your fingertips for pin bones, removing any that you find with tweezers. If the fillets are large, cut each across in half. Place the fillets skin-side up on a tray. Mix the saffron strands with 2 tablespoons olive oil and drizzle over the fish. Rub to adhere, then set aside to infuse for 5 to 10 minutes.

Meanwhile, heat 2 tablespoons olive oil in a saucepan and gently sauté the chopped red peppers for about 5 to 7 minutes until softened. Remove and set aside to cool.

Whiz half the red peppers in a food processor until smooth and creamy. Add to the mayonnaise and stir until well blended. Set aside.

Heat 4 tablespoons of the remaining oil in a frying pan and gently sauté the yellow pepper until softened, about 5 minutes. Add the chopped zucchini and eggplant, season, and cook for 5 to 10 minutes until the vegetables are tender.

Meanwhile, dip the tomato into a bowl of boiling water for a few seconds, then remove and slip off the skin. Halve, remove seeds and core, and finely dice the tomato flesh. Add to the ratatouille along with the remaining red pepper and the chopped basil. Check the seasoning.

When ready to cook, season the red mullet fillets with salt and pepper. Heat the remaining 2 tablespoons oil in a large, heavy-based frying pan over a high heat. When the pan is hot, add the fillets, skin-side down, and cook on this side only for about 3 minutes until the skin is really crisp. Take the pan off the heat and let rest for 5 minutes. The fish will be three-fourths cooked when you finish pan-frying—it will continue to cook as it rests.

Divide the ratatouille among warmed plates and top with the red mullet fillets. Thin the red pepper mayonnaise with a little water if necessary, then drizzle a little around each serving. Serve the rest separately.

4 small red mullet, about 8 oz (250 g)
  each, or 2 larger ones, about 1 lb
  (500 g) each, filleted (see below)
2/3 cup (150 ml) olive oil, plus extra
  for drizzling
large pinch of saffron strands
2 red bell peppers, cored, seeded,
  and finely diced
7 fl oz (200 ml) Mayonnaise
  (page 219)
1 yellow bell pepper, cored, seeded,
  and finely diced
1 large zucchini, finely diced
1 medium eggplant, finely diced
1 large plum tomato
1 tablespoon chopped basil
sea salt and freshly ground black pepper

TO FILLET RED MULLET
Lay the fish on a board and bend inward in a slight curve. With a sharp filleting knife, slit the skin from head to tail along the backbone, then cut across just below the head to the backbone. Starting at the head end and keeping the knife flat, skim it across the bones to detach the fillet. Turn the fish over and remove the second fillet in this way. Trim to neaten. If using two larger fish, cut the four fillets across in half. Don't discard the bones and heads—use to make stock.

sautéed cod with butternut squash purée

THIS DISH IS STUNNING—*the colors of the spinach and butternut purée offsetting the white cod flesh to perfection. Spinach is brilliant with fish, but you must avoid overcooking or cooking it in water as this would dilute the intense flavor. Butternut purée is a great alternative to potato.* SERVES 4 AS A MAIN DISH

4 cod steaks, about 4 oz (125 g) each

2 cups (300 g) peeled and roughly
   chopped butternut squash

1 thyme sprig, plus sprigs to garnish

½ stick plus 2 tablespoons (75 g)
   unsalted butter

4 tablespoons olive oil

about 7 oz (200 g) washed baby
   spinach leaves

sea salt and freshly ground black
   pepper

Preheat the oven to 400°F (200°C). Trim the fish steaks if necessary and set aside.

Put the squash into a medium pan and pour on sufficient boiling water to cover. Add the thyme sprig and simmer for 15 to 20 minutes until tender. Drain the squash and discard the thyme. Pass the squash through a mouli or purée in a blender or food processor until smooth. Add the half stick (50 g) butter and season generously with salt and pepper. Keep warm.

Heat half the olive oil with the remaining butter in a cast-iron skillet (large enough to take all 4 cod steaks) over a high heat. Add the fish, skin-side down, and cook for 3 minutes to sear the skin. Then turn the cod steaks over and cook for a further 1 to 2 minutes. Transfer the pan to the oven for 4 minutes to allow the fish to finish cooking while you sauté the spinach.

Heat the remaining 2 tablespoons olive oil in a medium pan, add the spinach leaves and cook, turning, for 1 to 2 minutes or until just wilted.

Place a mound of spinach in the center of each warmed large plate and position the cod, skin-side up, on top. Place a spoonful of the butternut squash puree to one side, garnish with thyme and serve immediately.

pan-fried salmon in a red wine sauce

SALMON IS MEATY ENOUGH *to take a smoky bacon and red wine sauce, especially if you accompany it with buttered spinach and a julienne of sweet, young carrots. I serve the fish with its crisp-fried skin uppermost, because it looks so tempting.*
SERVES 4 AS A MAIN DISH

Trim the salmon fillets to neaten if necessary, then score the skin (see below) and season it with salt and pepper; set aside.

To make the sauce, heat a large, wide pan until really hot, then add the olive oil and quickly sauté the bacon for 1 to 2 minutes until browned. Add the shallots along with the garlic and herbs, and cook until softened and caramelized, about 7 minutes. Deglaze with the port, then add the wine and cook until reduced by two-thirds. Pour in the two stocks and add pepper to taste. (You won't need salt because the bacon is salty.) Bring to a boil and simmer, uncovered, until reduced by half, about 15 to 20 minutes. Strain through a sieve, pressing with the back of a ladle. Set aside.

For the carrot julienne, cut the carrots into long, thin slices, then into very thin sticks. Heat half the butter in a pan and sauté the carrots for a minute or so. Add the chicken stock or water and a little seasoning. Simmer, uncovered, for about 3 minutes until the liquid is totally reduced and the carrots are glazed. Set aside; keep warm.

Heat 2 tablespoons olive oil and the remaining butter in a pan and sauté the spinach for a minute or two, until just wilted. Remove from the heat and season; keep warm.

To cook the salmon fillets, heat a nonstick frying pan until hot and add 1 to 2 tablespoons olive oil. Pan-fry the salmon, skin-side down, for 3 minutes. Flip over and cook the other side for 1 to 2 minutes. The flesh should be lightly springy when pressed; season lightly.

To serve, reheat the sauce. Place a mound of spinach in the center of each warmed plate and pour the sauce over it. Lay a salmon fillet, skin-side up, on top and finish with a little pile of carrot julienne. Drizzle a little olive oil around the sauce, if desired, and serve immediately.

4 thick-cut salmon fillets, about
  5 oz (140 g) each
2 carrots, peeled
3½ tablespoons (50 g) butter
½ cup (100 ml) Chicken Stock (page
  210) or water
4–5 tablespoons olive oil
about 7 oz (200 g) washed baby
  spinach leaves
sea salt and freshly ground black
  pepper

Sauce:
3 tablespoons olive oil
4 oz (100 g) diced Canadian bacon
1 large or 3 small shallots, minced
2 fat garlic cloves, chopped
1 thyme sprig
1 rosemary sprig
1 bay leaf
3 tablespoons port
½ cup (120 ml) red wine
1¾ cups (400 ml) Fish Stock
  (page 209)
2 cups (500 ml) Chicken Stock
  (page 210)

TO SCORE FISH SKIN *Use a razor-sharp knife, such as a craft knife or scalpel. Working across the grain of the skin, make shallow cuts just though to the flesh at ¼-inch (5-mm) intervals, leaving a ½-inch (1-cm) border at the edges.*

aromatic steamed cod

THICK, JUICY COD FILLETS *are steamed over water that is intensely flavored with a medley of spices, fresh herbs, and aromatics. The steam permeates the fish to impart a delicate, lingering flavor that is quite sensational. Naturally, the fish must be very fresh and thickly cut. Firm flesh is a good indicator—flesh that appears to be separating into flakes is beginning to stale. But if you can't find the best cod, then use chunky hake, haddock, or sea bass fillets instead. The steaming water can be reused: simply strain to remove the flavorings and refrigerate; use within a couple of days.* SERVES 4 AS A MAIN DISH

4 thick-cut cod fillets, about 6–7 oz
   (175–200 g) each
6 cups (1.5 liters) water
6 star anise
1 cinnamon stick
10 cardamom pods
10 whole cloves
1–2 tablespoons pink or Sichuan
   peppercorns
large handful of parsley sprigs
few large thyme sprigs
1 large bay leaf
3 shallots, sliced
½ head garlic
1 vanilla bean, split
1 lemon, cut into 6 slices
about 8 large lettuce leaves,
   to line steamer
few small basil sprigs
few tarragon sprigs
few rosemary sprigs
light olive oil, for drizzling
sea salt and freshly ground black pepper

Check the cod fillets for any residual bones by running your fingertips over the flesh. If you feel any, pull them out with your fingers or thin pliers. Wrap the fillets tightly in plastic wrap and chill. (If possible, leave them wrapped in the refrigerator overnight to set the shape.)

Put the water into a large pan that will take a large steamer. Add all the spices, the parsley, thyme, bay leaf, shallots, garlic, vanilla bean, and lemon slices. Bring to a boil, then lower the heat and simmer for 10 minutes. Take off the heat and set aside to infuse for an hour or so.

When ready to cook, unwrap the cod. Bring the water and aromatics back to a boil. Line the bottom of the steamer with lettuce leaves and scatter on the basil, tarragon, and rosemary. Place the cod on top and season with salt and pepper. Drizzle with olive oil.

Fit the steamer over the pan of simmering water, cover, and cook the fish fillets for 4 to 6 minutes. To test, check that the flesh feels firm when pressed, but take care as steam can easily scald. Lift the fish fillets onto warmed plates. Serve with a pilaff or plain boiled rice, and vegetables of your choice.

seared tuna with red chicory

I USE A PORTION CUT FROM THE TAIL END *of a whole tuna loin for this dish and marinate it overnight: Simply scatter thinly pared strips of orange and lemon zest over the tuna and sprinkle with coarse sea salt, then wrap in plastic wrap and leave in the refrigerator overnight. This simple technique really improves the texture of this meaty fish. Remember to bring it back to room temperature about half an hour before cooking. Alternatively, you can use ready sliced tuna steaks, as long as they are neatly trimmed and of even thickness.* SERVES 4 AS A MAIN DISH

4 tuna steaks, preferably freshly cut from
   the loin (tail end), about 4 oz (120 g)
   each and ½ inch (1 cm) thick

½ cup (100 ml) olive oil

2 tablespoons Dijon mustard

1 teaspoon honey

2 teaspoons soy sauce

6–8 tablespoons cracked black pepper

4 small heads of red chicory (treviso)
   or radicchio

confectioners' sugar, sifted, for dusting

1 lemon, quartered

If necessary, trim the tuna steaks. Mix half the olive oil with the mustard, honey, and soy sauce, and smear all over the steaks. Shake the pepper onto a sheet of wax paper. Press the steaks into the pepper until evenly coated.

Trim the ends of the red chicory and slice in half lengthwise. Set aside while you cook the tuna.

Heat 1 tablespoon of the remaining olive oil in a large frying pan until very hot and pan-fry the tuna steaks over a high heat for 45 seconds to 1 minute on each side; remove and set aside to rest while you cook the red chicory.

Preheat a large, heavy-based frying pan until almost smoking. Dust the red chicory liberally with sifted confectioners' sugar, then drizzle with the remaining olive oil. Place cut-side down in the pan and cook for about 1 to 1½ minutes, turning often, until they caramelize on the surface and start to wilt.

Divide the red chicory among warmed serving plates. Cut each tuna steak in half and place alongside. Squeeze on lemon juice to taste and drizzle any pan juices over the fish, then serve.

CARAMELIZING BITTER LEAVES *This is a great technique for sweetening bitter leaves, to serve as a warm salad. Halve small heads of red chicory, radicchio, or Belgian endive lengthwise; set aside for 5–10 minutes to let the bitter juices exude. Then sprinkle generously with sifted confectioners' sugar and drizzle with olive oil. Sear, cut-side down, in a smoking hot pan, and cook, turning often, until the leaves are just wilted and caramelized.*

skate with a sherry vinegar and caper sauce

SKATE IS A MISUNDERSTOOD AND UNDER-UTILIZED FISH. *Eaten fresh from the sea, it has an excellent taste and delicate texture. I like to cook it as fresh as possible with plenty of beurre noisette (browned butter). The addition of sherry vinegar and capers give this dish a real bite, I simply love it.* SERVES 4 AS A MAIN DISH

1 cup (250 ml) white wine

3 cups (750 ml) Fish Stock (page 209)

2 onions, finely chopped

2 carrots, chopped

1 celery stalk, chopped

6 parsley sprigs

4 thyme sprigs

2 bay leaves

10 black peppercorns

6 coriander seeds

2 star anise

1 small cabbage, cored and cut into
fine strips

1½ sticks (175 g) unsalted butter, cut
into pieces

2 tablespoons sherry vinegar

1 small tomato, skinned, seeded and
finely chopped

4 tablespoons capers, finely chopped

4 medium skate wings, skin removed

all-purpose flour, for coating

salt and freshly ground pepper

unsalted butter, for frying

Pour the wine and stock into a large pan, add the chopped vegetables, herbs and spices, and bring to a boil. Lower the heat and simmer for 10 minutes. Strain the stock to remove the flavorings, then add the cabbage to the pan. Bring to a boil, lower the heat, and cook for 5 to 10 minutes until tender but retaining a bite. Drain the cabbage and return to the pan, reserving the stock.

Strain the stock into a clean pan and boil until reduced to about 1 cup (250 ml) in volume. Gradually whisk in two-thirds of the butter, a small piece at a time, to make a glossy sauce.

Add 6 tablespoons of the sauce and 2 teaspoons of the sherry vinegar to the cabbage and toss to mix. Keep warm over a low heat.

Add the tomato, chopped capers, and the rest of the sherry vinegar to the sauce. Keep warm while you cook the skate, stirring frequently, but do not allow the sauce to become too hot or it will separate.

Season the flour lightly with salt and pepper, then toss the skate wings in the flour to coat evenly. Heat the remaining butter in a large skillet. Add two of the skate wings and pan-fry for 4 to 5 minutes each side. Remove to a warmed plate and keep warm while you pan-fry the other two skate wings, adding a little more butter to the pan if necessary.

To serve, divide the cabbage among warmed serving plates. Place the skate wings on top and pour over a little of the sauce. Serve the remaining caper sauce in a pitcher.

CHEF'S TIP *When making fine sauces, we tie flavoring vegetables and herbs in cheesecloth to make small bags before infusing in stocks. This prevents vegetable starches from leaching into the stock, so retaining its clarity. The cheesecloth bags are easily removed after infusing. The technique isn't essential here, but you may prefer to use it.*

sea bass baked on a bed of herbs

THIS IS A REALLY SIMPLE RECIPE, *but the flavors are superb. A whole sea bass is cooked on a lavish bed of herbs in a sealed foil package in the oven. Don't fail to savor the full aroma as you open the parcel—it is simply divine. Farmed sea bass is widely available, but I prefer to buy naturally caught fish that has a greater depth of flavor and looks so beautiful. You don't need to include all of the herbs listed below, but use at least four of them. The cooking juices make the accompanying sauce. To serve four, simply buy two fish and cook them in separate foil parcels. (Illustrated on page 42)* SERVES 2 AS A MAIN DISH

Rinse the inside of the fish well, making sure the central blood lines are washed away. Trim the tail and fins using scissors, then pat dry, inside and out. Score the skin of the bass on both sides, with the tip of a very sharp knife. Rub the skin with olive oil and season with salt and pepper. Tear off two large sheets of foil, each about 18 inches (45 cm) square and set aside.

Heat 1 tablespoon oil in a large, heavy-based frying pan. Lay the fish in the pan and fry briefly for about 30 seconds on each side to crisp the skin slightly. Remove from the heat.

Lay one of the foil squares on a clean surface. Scatter the herbs, lemon grass, and spices over the center of the foil sheet. Lay the whole sea bass on the herb bed. Drizzle with a little more olive oil and tuck the lemon slices around the fish.

Cover the fish loosely with the other square of foil and fold the edges together well to seal. The foil should form a roomy tent around the sea bass, allowing space for steam to surround and cook the fish. Place the foil parcel in a roasting pan and set aside in a cool place to infuse for 1 to 2 hours until ready to cook.

Preheat the oven to 350°F (180°C). Put the roasting pan in the center of the oven and bake for about 20 minutes until the fish is only just cooked.

Remove from the oven and let the fish rest, still wrapped, for about 5 to 10 minutes before serving. Unwrap the sea bass parcel at the table and spoon the tasty cooking juices over the fish as you serve it.

1 whole sea bass, about 1¾–2¼ lb (800 g–1 kg), scaled and gutted

1 tablespoon olive oil, plus extra for drizzling

4 bay leaves

handful of rosemary sprigs

handful of thyme sprigs

handful of tarragon sprigs

handful of basil sprigs

handful of sage sprigs

4–5 lemon grass stems, slit in half lengthwise

4 star anise

1 teaspoon mixed peppercorns

1 large lemon, thickly sliced and caramelized (see overleaf)

sea salt and freshly ground black pepper

monkfish in prosciutto

MONKFISH HAS BECOME INCREASINGLY POPULAR *and, as demand exceeds supply, so the price rockets. As a consequence, this superb, meaty fish is now one of the most expensive fish you can buy. It is the tail that we eat—the huge, bony head is discarded. The central cartilaginous bone that runs the length of the tail is removed to give two fillets. You will also need to remove the outer gray membrane, using a very sharp knife. Here, the monkfish fillets are wrapped in prosciutto and served on a bed of creamy cabbage with diced celeriac and carrots.* SERVES 4 AS A MAIN DISH

Using a sharp knife, remove as much as possible of the thin gray membrane that covers the fish. Fillet the monkfish by removing the central bone to give two meaty fillets.

Lay the prosciutto slices, slightly overlapping, on a surface lined with a sheet of plastic wrap. Place the two monkfish fillets in the middle, laying them side by side, but head to tail end. Wrap the prosciutto around the monkfish, making sure it is completely covered. Wrap the parcel tightly in plastic wrap. Twist the ends of the wrap to tighten the wrapping and chill for at least 1 hour—this helps set the shape. (You can do this a day in advance.)

Peel and dice the carrots and celeriac. Quarter the cabbage and remove the outer leaves. Cut out the core, then shred the cabbage finely. Bring a large pan of salted water to a boil. Have ready a large bowl of ice water.

Blanch the carrots and celeriac in boiling salted water for 2 minutes, remove with a slotted spoon, and refresh in cold water. Drain and set aside. Blanch the shredded cabbage in the same way, allowing 1 minute. Refresh in the ice water, then drain again.

When ready to cook the fish, preheat the oven to 350°F (180°C) (see right). Remove the plastic wrap from the monkfish parcel, then tie at intervals with string to hold the shape. Heat the olive oil and butter in a frying pan and, when it begins to foam, lower in the monkfish parcel. Cook, turning frequently, for 3 to 4 minutes until browned all over.

Lift the monkfish parcel into a baking dish, drizzle on the pan juices, and roast in the oven for 5 to 6 minutes until the fish is just firm. Remove from the oven and let rest in a warm place for 5 minutes.

Meanwhile, pour the cream into a large saucepan, bring to a boil, and bubble until reduced by half, then mix into the vegetables. Season to taste and cook for 1 to 2 minutes.

To serve, remove the string from the fish parcel, then cut into eight thick pieces. Divide the creamy vegetables among warmed serving plates and arrange the prosciutto-wrapped monkfish on top.

1 monkfish tail, about 1¼ lb (600 g)
about 5 oz (150 g) sliced prosciutto
2 large carrots
½ head celeriac
1 small head Savoy cabbage
about 2 tablespoons olive oil
3½ tablespoons (50 g) butter
1 cup (250 ml) heavy cream
sea salt and freshly ground black pepper

CHEF'S SECRET *If you find it more convenient to cook this dish entirely on the stovetop (and, like me, you are happy to use plastic wrap for steamed food), try the following method. It works brilliantly. Put the wrapped monkfish parcel in a steamer over boiling water, cover, and steam for 4 to 5 minutes. Remove from the steamer and let rest for 5 minutes, then remove the plastic wrap. Heat the butter and olive oil in a frying pan until foaming, add the monkfish, and pan-fry, turning, for 3 to 4 minutes until cooked.*

dover sole studded with herbs

I LIKE TO COOK AND SERVE DOVER SOLE *in a simple way to appreciate its fine flavor. For this dish I spike the fish with herb "cloutes" and cook it briefly on a grill pan, then roast the fish in foaming butter. It is best served simply too, with green beans or a salad. If Dover sole is unavailable or too expensive, you can use another sole, such as gray or Petrale, instead.* SERVES 2 AS A MAIN DISH

2 Dover soles, about 1 lb (500 g) each

2 large rosemary sprigs (preferably with woody stems)

12 large basil leaves

1 tablespoon olive oil

7 tablespoons (100 g) butter, in pieces

2 bay leaves

few thyme sprigs

splash of dry white wine

sea salt and freshly ground black pepper

Cut away the fins, then remove the dark skin and heads from the sole. Trim the tails. Rinse the fish gently and pat dry. Preheat the oven to 350°F (180°C).

Break the rosemary into smaller sprigs and wrap each sprig tightly in a basil leaf, to make 12 cloutes (see below).

Place the sole skinned-side up on a board and insert the stems of the herb cloutes into the fish. Heat the olive oil in a large frying pan or ridged grill pan and pan-fry the fish for 30 seconds on each side. Meanwhile, heat the butter in a small pan until melted and foaming.

Pour the foaming butter into a large baking pan and lay the Dover sole in the pan. Scatter the bay leaves and thyme sprigs on top of the fish and drizzle on the white wine. Season with salt and pepper. Bake for 8 to 10 minutes, basting the fish once or twice, until the flesh feels firm and flakes easily from the bone.

FLAVORING FISH WITH HERB CLOUTES *Choose woody rosemary or thyme sprigs and break into smaller sprigs. Slash the stem end of several large basil leaves. Wrap each rosemary or thyme sprig tightly in a basil leaf, starting from the tip of the basil leaf and leaving the woody herb stem protruding. Make small slits in the skin of the fish and insert these cloutes. If the fish is skinned, simply press the woody stems directly into the flesh. The herbs infuse the fish with their flavors during cooking and are easily removed before eating.*

TO SKIN DOVER SOLE *Lay the fish on a board, dark skin uppermost. Using the tip of a knife, loosen the skin near the tail and grasp it with salted fingers (so you can get a firm grip). Using your other hand to hold down the tail, pull the skin firmly, parallel with the fish, so that it comes away cleanly in one piece. The white skin can be removed in the same way, but if you are cooking the fish whole (as here) you'll find that leaving the white skin on helps keep the fish intact during cooking. (It can be removed easily after cooking.)*

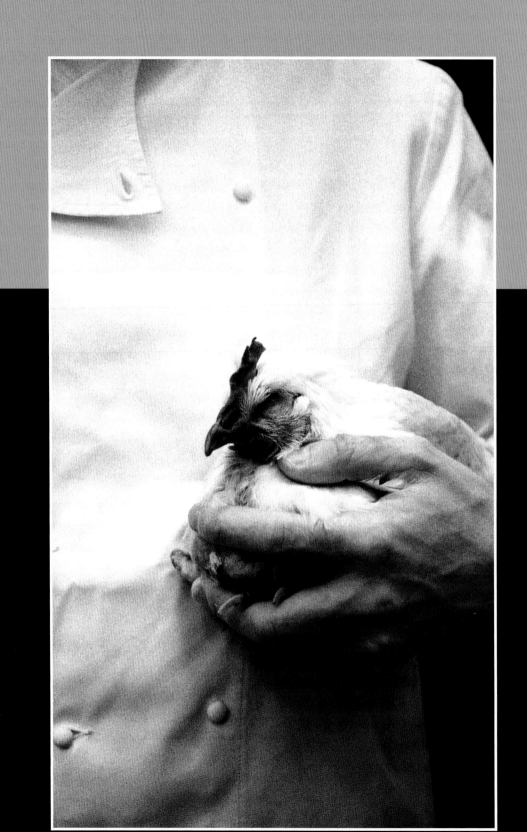

POULTRY AND GAME BIRDS

AT LAST, WE ARE BEGINNING *to respect the quality of poultry as they do in France. The French really love their poulet de Bresse and rigorously enforce high quality standards. I am pleased to see that many birds are now reared in true free-range conditions, giving us meat with a flavor and texture comparable to that of their French cousins. Norfolk-bred black leg chicken and the increasingly popular Gressingham duck are two of my favorites.*

We never roast a whole bird because the breast meat will become dry before the legs are cooked. A chef's trick, which ensures both white and brown meat is cooked to perfection, is to separate the legs from the main body. Breasts are roasted on the carcass as a "crown," moistened liberally with butter to help the skin to caramelize, while the legs are cooked separately—often boned and stuffed.

While I love cooking game birds, I hate shooting them. Other chefs may take up the sport and strut around looking macho with a shotgun, but I'm a bad shot. I stick to cooking them. Game birds can be a

roast chicken with herb butter

THE PROBLEM WITH ROASTING A LARGE CHICKEN *is that the breast and legs take different lengths of time to cook. Remove from the oven when the breast is juicy and tender, and the leg meat is invariably undercooked. Wait until the thigh meat is cooked and the breast will be dry. The trick is to cook them apart. Roast the legs separately to serve with the breast meat, or use for another recipe. Serve the chicken with creamy Pommes Dauphinoise (page 137) for the ultimate Sunday lunch.*

SERVES 4–6 AS A MAIN DISH

1 large free-range chicken, about
   4½ lb (2 kg)
¾ cup + 2 tablespoons (200 g) butter,
   softened
3 tablespoons chopped parsley
1 large carrot
1 large leek
1 onion
2 celery stalks
½ head of garlic, or 5 garlic cloves,
   peeled
handful of thyme sprigs
few small rosemary sprigs
1 lemon, halved
1 lb (500 g) baby carrots, with tops
6 cardamom pods
sea salt and freshly ground black pepper

To remove the chicken legs, slash the skin between the thighs and breast, pull the legs right out, and dislocate the joints, then cut through and separate the legs from the body.

Remove the wishbone to make the breast easy to carve: Lift up the neck skin to expose the wishbone and cut this away from the flesh, using a razor-sharp knife. Where the tip meets the breastbone, stick the knife tip in and smash down with your fist to break the bone for easy removal.

Preheat the oven to 375°F (190°C). Mix half the softened butter with the chopped parsley and season with pepper. Insert the herb butter between the breast skin and flesh (see below). The crown of chicken is now ready to roast.

Chop the large carrot, leek, onion, and celery and place in a roasting pan. Sit the chicken crown on top. Scatter the garlic cloves and herb sprigs over the surrounding vegetables. Season the chicken skin and place the two lemon halves in the body cavity.

Roast for about 30 minutes, basting the chicken with the pan juices three or four times, to help brown and crisp the skin. (The legs can be roasted separately; allow about 45 minutes.)

Meanwhile, trim the carrots, leaving on a little of the green stems. Melt the remaining butter in a heavy-based frying pan and cook the baby carrots with the cardamom pods and seasoning over a medium heat for about 15 minutes, turning occasionally, until tender and caramelized.

When the chicken breast feels firm, check that it is cooked: Insert a thin skewer into the thickest part; if the juices are clear it is done. If they are pink, roast for another 10 minutes or so.

Remove the crown to a warmed serving dish, cover with a loose "tent" of foil, and let rest for a good 15 minutes before carving. The juices will be reabsorbed into the meat, making it even more succulent. Carve the breast (and legs, if roasted at the same time). Serve with the cardamom carrots, and Dauphinoise potatoes, if desired.

STUFFING WITH HERB BUTTER *To keep the breast moist, spread herb butter under the skin. To do this, work your fingers under the breast skin to loosen it (working from either end), then insert the soft herb butter. Smooth the skin back in position, massaging to spread the butter evenly.*

butterflied cornish hens with sauce diable

BUTTERFLYING (OR BONING OUT) CORNISH HENS *before roasting or charcoal grilling speeds up the cooking process, which keeps the meat deliciously moist and succulent. Hell's kitchen style, I serve this with one of my favorite French sauces—sauce diable. Literally meaning the sauce of the devil, it's guaranteed to raise the temperature of any dinner party.*
SERVES 4 AS A MAIN DISH

4 small Cornish hens

2 tablespoons olive oil

4 small shallots, finely sliced

2 cups (225 g) fresh white bread
crumbs

1 tablespoon thyme leaves

1 tablespoon chopped parsley

¼ cup (50 g) unsalted butter

Sauce diable:

4 shallots, finely chopped

1¼ cups (300 ml) dry white wine

2 tablespoons white wine vinegar

2 cups (500 ml) Brown Chicken Stock
(page 210)

½–1 teaspoon cayenne pepper, or to
taste

Fried green tomatoes:

2 medium green tomatoes

1½ cups (175 g) all-purpose flour, plus
extra for dusting

1⅔ cups (250 g) cornmeal

¼ teaspoon cayenne pepper, or to taste

1 large egg

1 cup (250 ml) buttermilk

1 teaspoon baking powder

1½ teaspoons baking soda

vegetable oil for deep-frying

sea salt and freshly ground black
pepper

With a very sharp knife, cut down the backbone of each hen, and then carefully work around the carcass to remove it, severing the legs and wings and removing the thigh bone. Take care to keep the breast intact and don't pierce the skin. Preheat the oven to 400°F (200°C).

Heat the olive oil in a large skillet and pan-fry the hens on both sides until golden brown. Transfer to a large baking pan.

Add the shallots to the skillet and sauté until soft but not colored. Remove from the heat and mix with the bread crumbs and herbs. Sprinkle the crumb mixture over the chicken and press firmly.

Melt the butter in a small pan, then remove the scum from the surface. Pour the butter evenly over the hens and bake for 15 minutes. Remove from the oven and allow to rest for 15 minutes.

Meanwhile, make the sauce. Put the shallots, wine, and wine vinegar into a pan and bring to a boil. Let bubble over a medium-high heat until the liquid has reduced to a third of the original amount. Add the stock and continue to reduce until you have a sauce consistency. Season with enough cayenne to make a spicy sauce.

While the sauce is reducing, prepare the tomatoes. Cut them into ¼-inch (5-mm) thick slices and set aside. To make the coating, combine the flour, cornmeal, salt, pepper, and cayenne in a bowl. In another bowl, beat the egg with the buttermilk, baking powder, and baking soda.

Dust the tomato slices with flour. Then using tongs, dip them, one at a time, into the buttermilk mixture and then into the cornmeal mixture to coat. Place the tomato slices on a wire rack.

Heat the oil in a deep-fat fryer or deep, heavy saucepan until it registers 350°F (180°C) on a frying thermometer. Deep-fry the tomato slices in batches until crisp and golden. Remove and drain on paper towels.

Place the hens on warmed serving plates arrange the tomatoes around the birds and pour over a little sauce. Serve immediately.

poussin with turnips and white beans

I LIKE TO ROAST TENDER, BABY CHICKENS *and serve them with an interesting accompaniment. Here, baby turnips and white haricot beans in a chicken velouté—scented with chervil, chives, and truffle oil—fit the bill. You will need to soak the beans and prepare some velouté in advance. This is a really nice winter dish.* SERVES 4 AS A MAIN DISH

Soak the dried beans in cold water overnight, then drain and place in a saucepan. Add plenty of cold water to cover, bring to a boil, and add the onion, carrot, and bay leaf. Simmer for 1 hour or until just tender. Drain, refresh under cold running water, and drain again, discarding the flavorings. Season and set aside. Preheat the oven to 375°F (190°C).

Blanch the baby turnips in boiling water for a minute or so, then drain and refresh under cold running water. Peel the turnips thinly, cut into quarters, and season with salt and pepper.

Brush the chickens with the melted butter and season. Cover the breast of each with a small piece of foil. Roast for about 20 to 25 minutes until cooked. To check, pierce between the leg and breast: if pink juices run out, allow an extra 5 to 10 minutes in the oven.

Meanwhile, put the haricot beans and baby turnips into a saucepan with the velouté and bring to a boil. Simmer, uncovered, for 10 minutes or so, until the sauce is reduced by one-third. Check the seasoning and stir in the chopped herbs and truffle oil.

When the chickens are cooked, let them rest in a warm place for 10 minutes before serving. Strain the pan juices into a small saucepan and heat until bubbling, then whisk in the vinaigrette.

You can serve the birds whole, or cut up if you prefer (see below). Divide the velouté of turnips and white beans among warmed serving plates. Sit the chicken on top and drizzle the vinaigrette sauce over them.

⅔ cup (125 g) dried haricot or other
    white beans
1 small onion, sliced
1 small carrot, halved
1 bay leaf
16 baby turnips
4 poussins (squab chickens),
    14 oz–1 lb (400–500 g) each
about 3 tablespoons (40 g) butter,
    melted
1¼ cups (300 ml) Chicken Velouté
    (page 212)
1 tablespoon chopped chervil
1 tablespoon chopped chives
few drops of truffle oil
½ cup (100 ml) Vinaigrette
    (page 218)
sea salt and freshly ground black pepper

CHEF'S SECRET *Little chickens like this are often served whole, but I prefer to cut them up to make life easier for my guests. Using a sharp knife, cut through the thigh joint and remove the legs. We then pull out the thigh bone, leaving the drumstick in place, but you don't have to do this. Carefully cut the breasts from the bone in one piece and discard the carcasses. Arrange the whole breasts and legs on the plates.*

my chicken pie

A GREAT FAVORITE ON THE MENU AT CLARIDGES, *enjoyed by many of my guests. We bake the filling and pastry separately so the chicken remains succulent, and the pastry is light and crisp. You can either serve individual pies ready plated, as we do, or a whole pie in a traditional pie dish or baking dish (see below).* SERVES 4 AS A MAIN DISH

Cut the chicken into ¾-inch (2-cm) chunks. Dip the onions in boiling water for 30 seconds to loosen the skins, then remove and peel them. Bring the stock to a boil in a shallow pan, add the onions, and cook for 5 minutes. Lift out with a slotted spoon.

Add the chicken, bay leaf, and thyme to the stock. Return to a gentle simmer and poach for 5 minutes, then remove from the heat and let cool in the liquid for a minute or two. Strain the stock into a cup, discard the herbs, and season the chicken lightly; set aside.

Cut the pancetta into lardons (¾-inch/2-cm strips). Heat 2 tablespoons (25 g) of the butter in a frying pan or wok and stir-fry the pancetta until crisp, about 3 minutes. Remove and drain on paper towels. Wipe out the pan.

Melt the remaining butter in the pan. When it starts to foam, add the mushrooms and stir-fry for about 7 minutes until softened, seasoning to taste.

Pour in the sherry and bubble until well reduced. Return the bacon and onions to the pan and pour in the reserved stock. Bring to a boil and cook until reduced by half. Add the cream and bubble until reduced by one-third. Add the chopped herbs and set aside.

Heat the oven to 400°F (200°C). Roll out the pastry on a lightly floured surface to about ⅛ inch (3 mm) thick. Cut out four rounds, using a small saucer as a guide. Carefully place the pastry rounds on a large, nonstick baking sheet and score the surface in a diamond pattern, using the tip of a small, sharp knife.

Brush the pastry with the egg yolk glaze and bake for about 10 minutes until risen and golden. Bake for a further 2 minutes with the oven door slightly ajar, to help crisp the pastry. Remove from the oven and slide onto a wire rack.

Meanwhile, add the mushrooms to the sauce and reheat until bubbling, then add the chicken. As soon as the chicken is hot, check the seasoning and divide among warmed serving plates. Top each with a pastry round and serve.

4 skinless, boneless chicken breast
  halves, about 4 oz (120 g) each
4 oz (125 g) baby onions
2 cups (500 ml) Chicken Stock
  (page 210)
1 bay leaf
1 thyme sprig
7 oz (200 g) pancetta or Canadian
  bacon, in one piece
7 tablespoons (100 g) butter
8 oz (250 g) small button mushrooms
½ cup (100 ml) dry sherry
7 fl oz (200 ml) heavy cream
2 teaspoons chopped tarragon
1 tablespoon chopped parsley
8 oz (250 g) Puff Pastry (page 184)
1 medium egg yolk, beaten with
  1 teaspoon water
sea salt and freshly ground black pepper

TO SERVE AS A LARGE PIE *Prepare the filling as above. Cut out one large pastry crust to fit the top of a traditional English pie dish, or a baking dish, and place on a baking sheet. Cut the crust into quarters and move them apart slightly, then score, glaze, and bake as above. Tip the filling into the pie dish and assemble the crust on top.*

quail with a spiced honey dressing

I USE A POACHED-GRILLED TECHNIQUE TO COOK QUAIL *(illustrated on page 58) as this helps to keep the delicate meat succulent. Thereafter, I toss them with a spiced honey-mustard dressing and serve them on a bed of sauté potatoes with an arugula salad. Quail are now available from most good supermarkets as well as butchers. Allow two per person for a main course, one each for a first course. Most of the meat is on the breasts.* SERVES 4 AS A MAIN DISH

8 quail
4 cups (1 liter) Chicken Stock
  (page 210)
handful of thyme sprigs
8 small rosemary sprigs
finely pared zest of 2 limes, in strips
a little olive oil, for brushing
sea salt and freshly ground black pepper

Dressing:
6 tablespoons honey
1 tablespoon soy sauce
1 tablespoon coarse grain mustard
1 tablespoon Dijon mustard
1 tablespoon roasted sesame oil

Truss the quail by securing them with wooden toothpicks or simply by tying the legs together with string.

Pour the chicken stock into a medium saucepan, add the thyme sprigs, and bring to a boil. Add the quail, return to a simmer, and cook for 2 minutes. Remove and drain upside down in a colander. You may have to do this in two batches.

Pat the birds thoroughly dry with paper towels. Stuff the cavity of each quail with a rosemary sprig and a few lime zest strips.

Whisk the dressing ingredients together and set aside.

Heat a ridged grill pan (or the grill) until you can feel a steady, medium high heat—not too high or you will char the meat. Lightly oil the pan.

Brush the quail with a little olive oil and season lightly. Cook on the grill pan (or grill) for about 7 to 10 minutes, turning several times with tongs, until the birds are golden brown all over and the breasts are firm. Be careful not to burn the delicate meat.

Transfer the quail to a warmed, large, shallow bowl and pour on the dressing. Let marinate for 5 minutes, or a little longer. Untie the legs and remove the rosemary and lime zest from the cavities. Serve the quail on a bed of sliced sautéed potatoes with an arugula salad.

CHEF'S TIP *The stock will have taken on extra flavor from the quail, so don't discard it. Cool and use again—perfect for a velouté.*

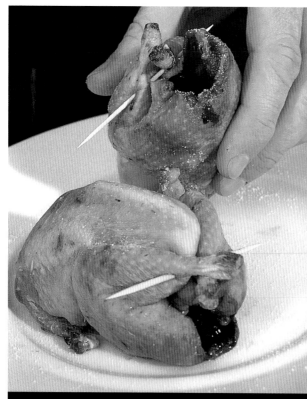

THE POCHE-GRILLE TECHNIQUE

Part poaching, part grilling is an excellent way to cook small birds, such as quail and squab, to keep them succulent. First, poach the quail in chicken stock to keep them moist as they partially cook. Then drain and pat dry with paper towels—the drier the skin, the crisper it will be. Finish cooking on a medium-hot grill or grill pan, turning with tongs to ensure the skin colors evenly. Should any part of the quail be slightly scorched, simply rub with a small cube of ice-cold butter. This helps to remove the charred bits.

chicken fricassée with peas and fava beans

A CLASSIC FRICASSÉE IS MADE BY POACHING CHICKEN *or veal in stock, then enriching the liquor with cream to make the perfect sauce. I like to sauté the chicken first, to give a better depth of flavor. For best results, buy a free-range or corn-fed chicken.* SERVES 4 AS A MAIN DISH

1 free-range chicken, about 3–4 lb (1.4–1.6 kg), cut into 8 pieces

4 tablespoons olive oil

5 tablespoons unsalted butter

2 carrots, chopped

2 celery stalks, chopped

1 onion, chopped

2 garlic cloves, chopped

3 Italian parsley sprigs

2 cups (500 ml) Chicken Stock (page 210)

½ cup (125 ml) dry white wine

½ cup (125 ml) heavy cream

1 cup (150 g) tiny pearl onions

4 oz (125 g) cured bacon, finely sliced

1 cup (150 g) frozen peas

1 cup (150 g) shelled baby fava beans

½ small romaine lettuce, finely sliced

3 tablespoons chopped chervil or parsley

sea salt and freshly ground black pepper

Season the chicken pieces with salt and pepper. Heat 3 tablespoons of the olive oil with 2 tablespoons of the butter in a Dutch oven, then fry the chicken, in batches, until golden on all sides. Remove with tongs and set aside.

Pour off most of the oil, then return the chicken to the pan. Add the carrots, celery, onion, garlic, and parsley sprigs. Pour in the stock and wine, and return to the heat. Bring to a boil, then lower the heat, and allow to simmer for 30 minutes.

Remove the chicken from the pan and set aside. Strain the broth through a fine sieve and return to the pan. Bring to a boil and boil to reduce by half. Skim off any fat from the surface. Add the cream and boil again, until thickened to a sauce-like consistency.

Heat the remaining olive oil and butter in a heavy pan. Add the pearl onions and sauté gently until softened, without coloring. Remove from the pan and set aside. Add the bacon to the pan and fry until crisp. Remove with a slotted spoon and drain on paper towel.

Return the chicken to the sauce and reheat gently, then add the pearl onions, bacon, peas, fava beans, and lettuce. Cook for a minute until the lettuce has just wilted. Check the seasoning and sprinkle with the chopped chervil. Serve immediately.

spiced chicken stew

I GET REAL SATISFACTION *out of creating tasty dishes using inexpensive cuts of meat and this aromatic stew is a prime example. Its origin dates back to colonial times. The British, who had acquired a taste for spices in India, introduced them to the southern states. This recipe was first created in the port of Savannah in Georgia and called "Country captain chicken stew."*
SERVES 4 AS A MAIN DISH

Heat 2 tablespoons of the olive oil in a large Dutch oven. Add the bacon and fry until crisp, then remove and drain on paper towel; set aside.

Season the flour with salt and pepper and toss the chicken pieces in the seasoned flour to coat.

Heat the fat remaining in the pan and sauté the chicken pieces in batches until the skin is golden brown in color, adding a little more oil if needed. Drain the chicken on paper towel and set aside with the bacon pieces.

Pour off excess fat from the pan if necessary, leaving a scant 2 tablespoons. Add the onion, peppers, and celery, and cook until soft, but not colored. Add the garlic, curry powder, ginger, thyme, paprika, allspice, cinnamon, and mustard seeds. Cook, stirring constantly, for 1 minute.

Add the cooked bacon pieces to the pan with the tomatoes, chicken stock, mango chutney, and lemon juice. Add the chicken pieces and simmer gently for 45 minutes or until the chicken is tender. Stir in the raisins and cream. Serve with plain rice.

3–4 tablespoons olive oil
5 oz (150 g) Canadian smoked bacon, cut in to ½-inch (1-cm) pieces
½ cup (50 g) all-purpose flour
8 chicken pieces, such as thighs and drumsticks
1 cup (125 g) chopped onion
1 cup (125 g) chopped red bell pepper
1 cup (125 g) chopped green bell pepper
1 cup (125 g) chopped celery
2 garlic cloves, chopped
2 tablespoons curry powder or garam masala
1-inch (2.5-cm) piece fresh ginger, peeled and grated
1 thyme sprig, leaves only
½ teaspoon paprika
¼ teaspoon allspice
¼ teaspoon ground cinnamon
¼ teaspoon mustard seeds
14½-oz (440 g) can plum tomatoes
1½ cups (375 ml) Chicken Stock (page 210)
¼ cup (4 tablespoons) mango chutney
2 teaspoons lemon juice
¾ cup (100 g) golden raisins
2 tablespoons heavy cream
sea salt and freshly ground black pepper

guinea hen with pomegranate

POMEGRANATES ARE POPULAR IN MIDDLE EASTERN COOKING, *and the juice is often used in meat and game dishes. Here, it is reduced to concentrate the flavor, then combined with vinaigrette, more pomegranate seeds, pink grapefruit, and walnuts, to make an original, fragrant dressing for full-flavored guinea hen. You could also serve quail or pheasant breasts in the same way.* SERVES 4 AS A MAIN DISH

3 ripe pomegranates

1 pink grapefruit

3 tablespoons cranberry juice

3 tablespoons freshly squeezed orange juice

6 tablespoons Vinaigrette, made with olive oil and walnut oil (page 218)

2 tablespoons freshly chopped walnuts

4 guinea hen breasts, about 4 oz (125 g) each

a little olive oil, for cooking

sea salt and freshly ground black pepper

Halve the pomegranates and carefully scoop out the seeds, discarding the membrane. Cut the peel and pith from the grapefruit, then cut out the segments using a small, sharp knife. Roughly chop the grapefruit flesh, reserving the juice.

Blitz two-thirds of the pomegranate seeds in a blender with the cranberry, orange, and reserved grapefruit juices, then strain through a sieve placed over a small pan, pressing with the back of a spoon. Boil to reduce by about half, until slightly syrupy, then add to the vinaigrette.

Pick over the rest of the pomegranate seeds, removing any stray membrane. Add to the dressing along with the grapefruit segments and chopped walnuts. Set aside.

Trim the guinea hen breasts to neaten, then rub the skin with olive oil and seasoning. Heat a heavy-based, nonstick frying pan and fry the breasts, skin-side down, for about 3 minutes. Turn the breasts over and cook the other side for 1 to 2 minutes. Do not overcook the meat—it should be very slightly pink.

Slice each guinea hen breast horizontally into three. Arrange on warmed plates, spooning the pomegranate dressing in between the slices. Serve with wilted spinach and sautéed potatoes.

PREPARING POMEGRANATES *Look for these reddish-yellow, hard-skinned fruits in markets in October and November. Use at the peak of ripeness, when the juice is at its sweetest. To prepare, halve vertically, then carefully spoon out the fleshy seeds. It is important to remove all of the creamy yellow membrane, which is very bitter.*

spiced duck with sweet-sour sauce

I RECOMMEND THAT YOU TRY SLOW-ROASTING DUCK LEGS *as a change from the more popular fast-roasted duck breasts. Duck legs also have a layer of fat under the skin, which bastes the meat during cooking to keep it moist. I use Gressingham ducks, a breed derived from mallard, which has a semi-gamy flavor. Here, the duck legs are roasted with aromatic spices and served with a Spanish-style citrus and sherry vinegar sauce.* SERVES 4 AS A MAIN DISH

4 duck legs
1 teaspoon ground coriander
1 teaspoon ground mace
1 teaspoon ground ginger

Sweet-sour sauce:
2 tablespoons (25 g) sugar
2 tablespoons honey
⅔ cup (150 ml) sherry vinegar
juice of 2 oranges
juice of 2 lemons
pan juices from the roasted duck legs
1 tablespoon (15 g) butter
sea salt and freshly ground black pepper

Stab the skin of the duck legs a few times with a fine skewer. Mix all the spices together and rub into the legs. Place the duck in a dish and let marinate in the refrigerator for about 2 hours.

Preheat the oven to 350°F (180°C). Place the duck legs, skin-side up, in a roasting pan and roast for 45 to 50 minutes. There is no need to baste them during roasting; simply turn once or twice, then roast undisturbed to let the skin become really crisp. Pour off the fat halfway through cooking (but don't discard, see below).

When the duck legs are very tender, transfer to a warmed plate and let rest, uncovered, in a warm place. For the sauce, sprinkle the sugar into the meat juices in the roasting pan and add the honey. Cook on the stovetop, stirring with a wooden spoon, until nicely caramelized.

Deglaze with the sherry vinegar and bubble until reduced by half. Stir in the orange and lemon juices and bubble again until reduced by half. Strain the sauce through a fine sieve into a bowl and beat in the butter. Season with salt and pepper to taste.

Serve the duck legs with the sweet-sour sauce. Crisp, sautéed potatoes and a watercress salad are good accompaniments.

DUCK FAT *We use this all the time in our restaurants, especially for our famous confit recipes (see right). A lot of fat is released when you roast a duck (or portions). It has a good flavor and is worth saving. At home, I strain the duck fat through a sieve lined with paper towel, then store it in a covered jar in the fridge It is excellent for roasting and sautéeing potatoes. The duck fat can be kept in the fridge for up to 2 weeks, but should then be discarded.*

confit of duck in savoy cabbage

THIS SLOW METHOD OF COOKING *dates back to the dawn of French cuisine. It was originally used a way of preserving meat, but it is now a popular technique, used in top restaurants all over the world. The duck is cooked very slowly, immersed in goose or duck fat, until it is meltingly tender. Make sure you buy full-flavored duck.* SERVES 4 AS A MAIN DISH

Press the thyme leaves on to the skin of the duck and then sprinkle well with sea salt. Leave at room temperature for 1 hour to draw out some of the moisture.

Preheat the oven to 300–325°F (150–160°C). Transfer the duck legs to an ovenproof dish in which they fit quite snugly. Warm the goose or duck fat until it is hot, about 210°F (100°C), but do to allow it to boil.

Pour the fat evenly over the duck legs, and add the bay leaf and parsley. Place in the warm oven and leave to confit for 3 to 4 hours.

Remove from the oven and allow the duck to cool in the fat. When cold, remove the duck legs from the fat and drain on paper towel. Strip off the skin and discard, then remove the meat from the bones. Strain the fat and reserve for other uses (see below). Set the duck confit aside.

Using a sharp knife, remove the core from the cabbage, then carefully remove eight large outer leaves, keeping then whole. Bring a pan of water to a boil, add the whole leaves, and blanch for 2 to 3 minutes. Drain and refresh in a bowl of cold water. Drain and dry on paper towels, then lay the cabbage leaves on a clean surface and divide the duck confit between them. Carefully roll up the leaves to enclose the filling and set aside.

Finely slice the rest of the cabbage. Heat the butter in a skillet and sauté the cabbage for 3 to 4 minutes until just wilted. At the same time, gently warm the cabbage parcels in a steamer.

Place two parcels on each warmed plate and spoon the sautéed cabbage alongside. Spoon some of the red wine sauce over the parcels and serve the rest separately, in a pitcher.

Confit of duck legs:
leaves from 1 thyme sprig
freshly ground sea salt
4 duck legs
2 cups (500 g) goose or duck fat
1 bay leaf
few parsley stalks

For serving:
1 medium Savoy cabbage
2 tablespoons (25 g) unsalted butter
Red Wine Sauce (page 213)

THE CONFIT TECHNIQUE
This is used on a daily basis in my restaurants, and it isn't solely reserved for duck. We apply it to all sorts of ingredients, even vegetables, such as potato and fennel, and cherry tomatoes. Lamb and fish, like salmon and trout, confit well. The duck fat used for confit has a fabulous flavor so we never discard it. After straining it can be kept in the fridge and used for roasting potatoes.

MEAT

WHEN I REFLECTED ON MY CHOICE *of recipes for this chapter, I realized just how many of my dishes are moving toward the rustic. I love the challenge of taking so called "poor" cuts and turning them into superlative meals. Fresh pork belly, beef shank, and lamb shanks can be transformed into dishes fit for a new rich man. And, of course, we have a generation of new young diners who have been brought up on quick-cook cuts of meat, many of whom have never had the opportunity to enjoy country-style dishes.*

Slow-roast pork and lamb crépinettes are a revelation—full of flavor, fork-tender, and presented in a way that rivals many great haute cuisine classics. I won't pretend these are quick to prepare, but they are certainly not difficult to cook if you follow the recipes and techniques I give in this chapter.

Naturally, I appreciate the finer top cuts and look to ways to cook—and serve—them to perfection. Take meltingly tender filet mignon steaks and succulent calf's liver, for example. Here, I pan-sear the steaks ahead and top them with a gratin of mushrooms, ready to finish cooking in a hot oven to serve. Yes, it is possible to do this and serve the meat piping hot and rare. As for calf's liver, forget slicing it thinly to flash fry, let alone dusting it with flour—the sure way to end up with hard, leathery liver. Instead, cut it the thickness of a sirloin steak and cook until pink and juicy, to serve alongside pan-fried polenta.

braised pork in a rich glaze

THIS SPECTACULAR DISH REGULARLY APPEARS ON MY MENUS. *Country-style ribs may be a cheaper cut, but it responds beautifully to slow, gentle cooking, becoming meltingly tender. You may need to order this cut in advance from your butcher, or look for it in Asian markets. I like to serve this with truffle-scented Pomme Purée (page 136), lightly wilted spinach, and steamed asparagus spears.* SERVES 4 AS A MAIN DISH

2¼ lb (1 kg) country-style pork ribs

4 tablespoons olive oil

1 carrot, chopped

1 onion, chopped

1 leek, chopped

1 celery stalk, chopped

½ head garlic or 6 fat garlic cloves, peeled

½ cup (100 ml) sherry vinegar

7 fl oz (200 ml) soy sauce

6 cups (1.5 liters) Brown Chicken Stock (page 210)

5 star anise

20 coriander seeds

10 white peppercorns

10 black peppercorns

To prepare the pork, use a sharp filleting knife to cut off the skin, leaving a thin layer of fat about ¼ inch (5 mm) thick. Remove the rib bones and discard. Even out the thickness by taking a slice from any thicker areas and placing where the meat is thinner. You should now have an even sheet of boned pork belly. Roll this up quite firmly and tie into a neat, even-shaped roll (see overleaf).

Heat a shallow, cast-iron casserole or deep sauté pan (with lid) until you feel a strong heat rising. Add 2 tablespoons olive oil, then brown the pork roast, turning until caramelized all over. Remove to a plate.

Add the remaining olive oil to the pan and sauté the vegetables and garlic for about 5 minutes. Deglaze with the sherry vinegar and cook until reduced by half. Return the pork to the pan, placing it on top of the vegetables.

Pour in the soy sauce and stock, then add the whole spices. Bring to a boil and partially cover the pan. Braise slowly over a low heat, or in the oven at 325°F (170°C), for 2½ to 3 hours, basting occasionally with the pan juices, until the meat feels very tender. To test, push a metal skewer into the middle of the roast; there should be little resistance.

Lift out the pork and set aside to rest on a warmed plate. Strain the pan juices into a pan and bubble to reduce to a glossy brown glaze.

To serve, remove the string and cut the pork roll into portions, or thick slices. Arrange on warmed plates and surround with wilted spinach and asparagus. Serve with pomme purée.

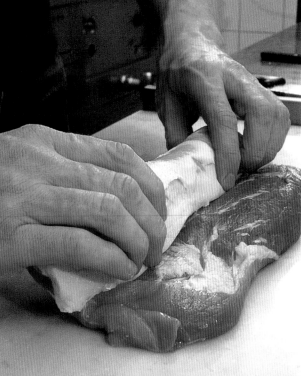

TO TIE A ROLLED ROAST *First, cut a long piece of kitchen string and tie the roast lengthwise, leaving at least 4 inches (10 cm) on one end of the string. Then tie a piece of string around one end of the roll and knot firmly. Next, cut a long piece of string and tie to one end of the knot you have just made. Pull it along about 1½ inches (3 to 4 cm) and loop around the meat, pulling the string through once but not knotting. Repeat by pulling and looping at about 1½-inch (3- to 4-cm) intervals until you reach the end of the roll. Tie the string to the loose end (from the first tying).*

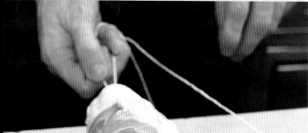

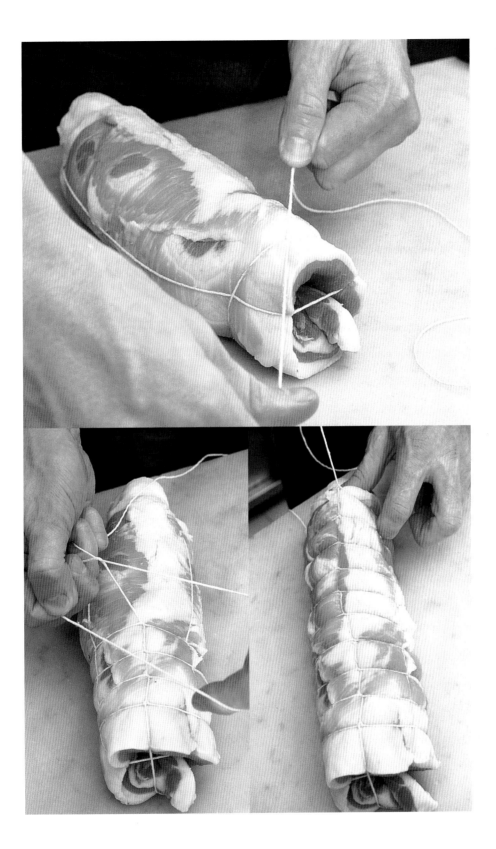

filet mignon with wild mushrooms

THIS IS A GREAT WAY TO COOK THICK, JUICY FILET MIGNON STEAKS. *You do need prime quality, thick cut steaks from a neat, round tenderloin, which can only come from a good butcher who cuts to order. For convenience, the steaks can be seared and topped with the mushrooms in advance, ready to finish in a hot oven just before serving—ideal if you are entertaining.*
SERVES 4 AS A MAIN DISH

Prepare the topping ahead: Gently sauté the shallot and garlic in 1 tablespoon olive oil for about 5 minutes until nicely softened.

Add a further 2 tablespoons olive oil and sauté the mushrooms over a high heat, stirring frequently, for about 7 minutes until browned and cooked. Add the wine and cook until it has reduced away. The mixture should be quite dry. If necessary, tip it into a strainer to drain off any remaining liquid. Transfer the mushrooms to a bowl, season, and mix in the herbs. Let cool.

Whip the cream until softly stiff, then fold into the mushrooms along with the egg yolk. Cover and chill.

Brush the steaks with the remaining tablespoon of olive oil and season them. Heat a large, nonstick frying pan until you can feel a strong heat rising. Cook the steaks for about 2 to 3 minutes, turning them to sear all over. Remove from the pan, season, and let cool.

When ready to serve, heat the oven to 425°F (220°C). Put the steaks on a shallow baking pan. Pile the mushroom mixture on top of the steaks and dust with Parmesan. Cook, uncovered, for about 5 to 7 minutes until the topping is bubbling and golden. Serve as soon as possible, with roasted or sautéed potatoes and a salad.

1 shallot, minced

1 fat garlic clove, crushed

4 tablespoons olive oil

4 oz (100 g) fresh wild mushrooms (such as chanterelles or morels), or shitake or oyster mushrooms, trimmed and minced

1½ cups (100 g) chopped crimini mushrooms

2 tablespoons white wine

1 tablespoon each minced parsley, chervil, and chives

4 tablespoons heavy cream

1 extra large egg yolk

4 filet mignon steaks, about 6 oz (180 g) each and 1½ inches (4 cm) thick

2 tablespoons freshly grated Parmesan cheese

sea salt and freshly ground black pepper

CHEF'S SECRET *For this dish, we buy a whole beef tenderloin, weighing approximately 1¼ lb (600 g). To prepare, we trim the ends and cut away any sinews, then wrap the tenderloin tightly in plastic wrap and chill it overnight. This helps to set the shape, to give you perfectly round steaks.*

beef tenderloin with baby artichokes

FOR A VERY SPECIAL ROAST, *I buy a whole beef tenderloin and cook it simply in foaming butter. Serve with sautéed artichoke hearts and a creamy, horseradish-flavored Pomme Purée (page 136). Trickle the irresistible buttery juices over the beef slices and you won't need to make a sauce.* SERVES 4 AS A MAIN DISH

1 whole, thick beef tenderloin roast,
  about 1¼ lb (600 g)
16 baby globe artichokes, or 4 large
  ones
juice of 1 lemon
5 tablespoons olive oil
4½ tablespoons (70 g) lightly salted
  butter, cut into small cubes
sea salt and freshly ground black pepper

Check that the membrane has been removed from the beef—this is visible as a silvery film. Use a razor-sharp filleting knife to remove it, if necessary. Wrap the tenderloin tightly in plastic wrap, rolling it a few times and twisting the ends tightly to seal. Chill for at least 4 hours, preferably overnight, to set the shape.

Meanwhile, prepare the artichokes. Remove the outer leaves and hairy choke to expose the hearts, dropping them into a bowl acidulated with half the lemon juice as you do so. If large, cut the hearts into quarters. Put into a shallow pan and add the remaining lemon juice and just enough water to cover. Bring to a boil, then lower the heat and simmer for about 15 to 20 minutes until tender.

When ready to cook, unwrap the beef and season. Preheat the oven to 350°F (180°C). Use a sauté pan that you can put into the oven. (If you do not have a suitable pan, put a small roasting pan in the oven to heat.)

Heat the sauté pan (or a frying pan) until you can feel a good heat rising. Add 2 tablespoons olive oil and brown the beef tenderloin, turning it until evenly caramelized. This should take about 5 minutes.

Add the butter gradually and let it foam, then spoon over the meat. Place the pan in the oven (or transfer the beef to the hot roasting pan and pour the butter over it). Roast for 20 minutes, spooning the butter over the meat at least twice in that time. Press the meat with the back of a fork: it should feel lightly springy. If it feels quite soft, baste well and give it another 5 minutes in the oven.

Transfer the beef to a warmed plate, reserving the pan juices, and let rest in a warm place for 5 minutes while you finish the artichokes: Heat the remaining olive oil in a frying pan. Drain the artichokes and sauté in the hot oil until golden brown and crisp on the outside. Season and remove from the heat.

Strain the buttery pan juices from the meat through a fine sieve and reheat. Cut the beef into eight even slices and place two on each warmed dinner plate, adding any juices from carving to the pan juices. Surround the beef with the artichokes and drizzle with the juices. Serve with horseradish pomme purée.

CHEF'S SECRET *We clarify butter for many uses, but not when the dish calls for foaming butter. The milky solids (or impurities) in the butter encourage it to foam, so the last thing you want to do is remove them.*

A CUT ABOVE THE REST *For melting tenderness, you cannot surpass a good beef tenderloin. I strongly recommend that you buy from a specialty butcher, rather than a supermarket. Flavor is all-important, so make sure the tenderloin is from an animal that has been hung for at least 3 weeks.*

roast lamb with mushroom and spinach stuffing

THIS IS PERFECT FOR A SPECIAL SUNDAY LUNCH *and easy to prepare—especially if you get your butcher to bone the lamb for you. You'll need a medium leg boned out flat (rather than tunnel-boned), with is sometimes called butterflying. Use the bones to make stock and reduce to concentrate the flavor—the basis for a delicious gravy. Serve with potatoes roasted in goose fat and flageolet beans tossed in a little butter and parsley.* SERVES 6 AS A MAIN DISH

Bone the lamb so that it opens out flat (or get your butcher to do this) and spread it on a board, skin-side down. Using a sharp knife, cut out any sinews or excess fat and trim away 5 oz (150 g) of meat. Put this in a food processor and whiz to a purée. Add the cream, ½ teaspoon salt, and some pepper, and blend briefly until smooth. Turn into a bowl, cover, and refrigerate, with the lamb.

Mince the mushrooms very finely. Heat the butter in a frying pan and sauté the shallot or onion and garlic for about 3 minutes until softened. Add the minced mushrooms and fry, stirring, over a high heat until softened and browned, about 7 minutes. Season well, then let cool.

Blanch the spinach in boiling water for 1 minute, then drain and plunge into a bowl of ice water to refresh. Drain thoroughly and squeeze dry, then mince and mix with the mushrooms and tarragon. The mixture should be quite dry. If necessary, wrap in cheesecloth and squeeze out any liquid. Add the spinach and mushrooms to the lamb purée and check the seasoning (see Chef's Tip).

Lay the lamb flat on a clean surface and spread the stuffing evenly over the inside, then roll up firmly and tie at intervals with kitchen string to secure. If necessary, sew any open edges together with a trussing needle and thread. Roll the neat stuffed roast tightly in plastic wrap and refrigerate for a couple of hours to help set the shape.

Preheat the oven to 350°F (180°C). Unwrap the lamb and weigh to calculate the cooking time: Allow 50 minutes per 2¼ lb (1 kg) for medium rare meat and 55 minutes per 2¼ lb (1 kg) for medium. Add 12 minutes for each additional 8 oz (250 g). Place the lamb in a roasting pan, drizzle with a little olive oil, and sprinkle with seasoning. Lay parchment paper on top to prevent overbrowning. Roast the lamb for the calculated time—around 1¾ to 2 hours—basting every 30 minutes with the meat juices.

Transfer the meat to a platter and let rest in a warm place for 15 minutes or so. Strain the juices into a small saucepan, add the stock, wine, and rosemary, and bubble for a few minutes to reduce down, then strain into a gravy boat. Carve the meat into fairly thick slices, tipping any juices that seep out into the gravy boat. Serve the meat with the gravy.

1 leg of lamb, about 5–5½ lb (2.3–2.5 kg)

2 tablespoons heavy cream

8 oz (250 g) fresh mushrooms, wild or cultivated (or a mixture), trimmed and cleaned

4½ tablespoons (70 g) butter

1 shallot, or ½ onion, minced

1 fat garlic clove, chopped

8 oz (250 g) washed baby leaf spinach

1 tablespoon chopped tarragon

a little olive oil, for drizzling

1¼ cups (300 ml) well-flavored reduced lamb stock

⅔ cup (150 ml) red wine

few rosemary sprigs

sea salt and freshly ground black pepper

CHEF'S TIP *Tasting a stuffing that contains raw meat to check the seasoning is never a good idea, yet it's important to get this right. I fry off a teaspoonful of the stuffing in a little oil until just firm, then taste it and adjust the stuffing seasoning accordingly.*

lamb crépinettes in lettuce

LAMB SHANKS ARE BRAISED SLOWLY *to give very tender meat, which is then shredded and enriched with some of the braising liquid and flavorings. This is pressed into balls, wrapped in blanched lettuce leaves, and poached. An impressive and unusual main course, it is best served on a creamy parsnip purée with roasted root vegetables, and steamed asparagus and baby leeks.*
SERVES 8 AS A MAIN DISH

olive oil, for frying
4 lamb shanks
1 carrot, roughly chopped
1 onion, roughly chopped
1 leek, roughly chopped
1 celery stalk, roughly chopped
½ head garlic, or 6 fat garlic cloves
1 thyme sprig
1 bay leaf
1 rosemary sprig
2 star anise
4 cardamom pods
8 black olives
1¼ cups (300 ml) dry white wine
6 cups (1.5 liters) Brown Chicken Stock
    (page 210)
18 romaine leaves (from about
    4 lettuce hearts)
sea salt and freshly ground black pepper

For steaming:
2 bay leaves
2 thyme sprigs
1 teaspoon coriander seeds

Heat a large frying pan until you can feel a strong heat rising, then add a little olive oil and brown the shanks all over, turning frequently. Remove and set aside.

Heat a little more olive oil in the pan, add the chopped vegetables and garlic, and sauté for 5 minutes to soften. Add the herbs, whole spices, and 4 olives. Pour in the wine and boil until reduced right down to a thin syrup.

Transfer the vegetable mixture to a large, cast-iron casserole or heavy-based saucepan with a tight-fitting lid and place the lamb shanks on top. Pour in the stock and bring to a simmer. Season, then cover and cook at a very gentle simmer for 2½ to 3 hours until the meat is very tender. Leave in the liquid for 30 minutes, then transfer to a dish using a slotted spoon and cool completely. Strain the liquid into a shallow pan, discarding the vegetables and flavorings, then boil rapidly until reduced to a rich glaze, about 1½ cups (350 ml); set aside.

Pick the meat from the bones and snip off any sinews. Now pull the meat into fine shreds with your fingertips and place in a bowl. Chop the rest of the olives and add to the lamb with 7 fl oz (200 ml) of the glaze. Mix well and check the seasoning, then chill. Reserve the remaining glaze.

When ready to shape the crépinettes, blanch the lettuce leaves, a few at a time, in a large pan of boiling water for about 5 seconds until wilted. Lift out with a slotted spoon and refresh in a bowl of ice water. Remove, drain, and pat dry with paper towels.

Divide the meat into 8 portions. Roll neatly into balls, but don't press too firmly. Lightly oil a medium ladle and line it with 3 blanched leaves, overlapping the leaf tips in the center and letting the stem ends hang over the edge. Place a lamb ball in the middle and fold over the overhanging leaves, pressing lightly to mold. Repeat with the remaining balls and lettuce leaves to make 8 crépinettes. Chill on a plate, join-side down.

When ready to serve, add the bay leaves, thyme, and coriander seeds to a large pan of boiling water. Place parchment paper on the bottom of a bamboo steamer (that fits the pan) and place the wrapped lamb balls on top. Position on the steamer pan, cover, and cook for about 12 minutes until piping hot. In the meantime, reheat the remaining glaze. Serve the crépinettes on a bed of creamy parsnip purée, surrounded with vegetables and drizzled with the glaze.

tomatoes stuffed with chili beef

REAL DICED BEEF, PLENTY OF CHILI AND A HINT OF CUMIN *take the chili back to its no-frills Texan origin. The twist is that we serve it in a hollowed-out beef tomato, just the ticket to serve to the boys when they are watching the next Superbowl.* SERVES 4 AS A MAIN DISH

5 tablespoons peanut oil

1 onion, finely chopped

1½ tablespoons chili powder

1 tablespoon toasted cumin seeds

2 teaspoons dried oregano

2 lb (1 kg) beef chuck roast, cut into
　　½-inch (1-cm) cubes

¼ cup (50 g) diced Canadian
　　smoked bacon

1 tablespoon tomato paste

2 cups (425 g) crushed tomatoes

1¾ cups (450 ml) beef stock

4 large beef tomatoes, blanched and
　　peeled (see below)

4 teaspoons sour cream

2 tablespoons roughly chopped cilantro

salt and freshly ground black pepper

Heat 2 tablespoons of the peanut oil in a Dutch oven. Add the onion, chili powder, cumin seeds, and oregano, and cook over a medium-low heat, stirring occasionally, for 5 minutes.

Add the remaining oil and increase the heat to high. Brown the meat and bacon, in two batches if necessary, turning to color evenly.

Stir in the tomato paste, crushed tomatoes, and stock, season well, and bring to a simmer. Cook for 2 hours, covering with the lid when the mixture becomes thick.

Meanwhile, preheat the oven to 400°F (200°C). Cut the tops off the beef tomatoes and scoop out the core and seeds, using a teaspoon. Fill the beef tomatoes with the chili beef. Place in the oven for 2 to 3 minutes to heat through.

To finish, top each stuffed tomato with a teaspoon of sour cream, and sprinkle with the cilantro. Serve immediately.

BLANCHING AND PEELING TOMATOES *In the restaurants, there is always a pan of boiling water on the stove ready for blanching, but at home you will need to bring a large pan to a boil. Using a sharp knife, cut out the top of the tomato where the stalk has been attached. Have ready a large bowl filled with ice water. Place the tomatoes in the boiling water and leave for 2 to 3 minutes, then remove with a slotted spoon and immediately plunge into the ice water. Allow to cool in the water for 4 to 5 minutes, then remove and peel away the skin.*

veal and foie gras meat loaf with tomato relish

THE VEAL AND FOIE GRAS BURGER *on the menu of my London-based American-style café is so popular that my customers won't let me take it off! Here I have adapted it to make a classic family favorite meat loaf, and served it with a delicious homemade tomato relish.* SERVES 6 AS A MAIN DISH

Preheat the oven to 350°C (180°C). Finely chop the foie gras and combine with the ground meat and shallots. Season very generously with salt and pepper, then add the thyme and parsley. Add enough egg to bind the mixture, using your hands to work the ingredients together thoroughly.

Pack the mixture into a 2 lb (900 g) loaf pan and level the surface. Bake in the oven for 45 minutes.

To make the tomato relish, peel the tomatoes (see left) and chop roughly. Place in a heavy-based pan with the sugar, cider vinegar, salt, and pepper. Wrap the allspice, cloves, coriander seeds, and mustard seeds in a square of cheesecloth and tie securely with string. Add the spice bag to the tomatoes. Bring to a boil, then lower the heat and simmer for 30 minutes, stirring frequently. Allow to cool slightly, then remove the spice bag. Pass the tomato mixture through a chinois or strainer into a nonmetallic bowl. (The relish can be prepared ahead and kept in the refrigerator for up to 1 week).

When the meat loaf is cooked, remove from the oven and allow to stand in the pan for 5 minutes.

Turn the meat loaf out onto a warmed serving dish. Cut into slices and serve at once, with the tomato relish.

12 oz (350 g) prepared foie gras
1¼ lb (550 g) lean ground veal
  or pork
3 small shallots, minced or finely sliced
4–5 thyme sprigs, leaves only
1 tablespoon chopped parsley
1 medium egg, beaten
sea salt and freshly ground black
  pepper

Tomato relish:
1½ lb (700 g) ripe tomatoes
1 cup (200 g) sugar
½ cup (125 ml) cider vinegar
1 teaspoon salt
½ teaspoon freshly ground black
  pepper
6 allspice berries
6 cloves
6 coriander seeds
¼ teaspoon mustard seeds

CHEF'S TIP *The secret of success here is to season the meat loaf mixture liberally with salt and pepper. If in doubt, fry off a teaspoonful of the mixture in a little oil, then taste to check the seasoning, and add more to the mixture if needed.*

CHEF'S SECRET *To retain its silky texture and delicate flavor, cook calf's liver as you would a filet mignon steak, rather than in thin slices, which overcook in mere seconds. Let the liver rest for 5 minutes after cooking, to firm up before serving.*

calf's liver with fried polenta

CALF'S LIVER HAS A FINE, DELICATE TEXTURE *that is easily toughened if you cook it in thin slices—the best way to ruin it in my view. I prefer to pan-fry thicker "steaks," which then get a better "cuisson" and so retain their sweet succulence to delicious effect. Ask your butcher to cut you a thick piece of liver and portion it at home. Crisp-fried wedges of polenta are the perfect accompaniment. And to continue the Italian theme, I make a dressing with crushed fresh figs. Mouthwateringly good!*
SERVES 4 AS A MAIN DISH

First, make the polenta: Put the milk, water, olive oil, thyme, and 1 teaspoon salt into a large, deep pan. Bring to a boil. Trickle in the polenta as you stir briskly with a long-handled spoon held in your other hand. Always stir in one direction to avoid lumps forming. The mixture will thicken fairly quickly and start to splutter a bit. Don't be tempted to cover the pan as you need to stir the polenta. Cook for 15 to 20 minutes over a low heat, stirring frequently.

Remove from the heat and stir in the butter and Parmesan, then tip the polenta into a shallow tray and spread to a depth of about ⅝ inch (1.5 cm). Leave until cool and set, about 1 hour, then cut into wedges. Allow two or three wedges per serving. (Wrap any that you don't need in plastic wrap and refrigerate; use within 3 days.)

To make the dressing, break open 2 figs and scrape out the flesh into a bowl, breaking it up with a fork. Gradually mix in the vinaigrette, then set aside.

Trim any tubes or membrane from the liver, then cut into four portions. Cut the remaining figs in half lengthwise. Set aside while you cook the polenta wedges.

Dust each polenta wedge with flour that has been seasoned with salt and pepper. Heat a ¼-inch (5-mm) depth of olive oil in a large frying pan. When hot, fry the polenta for about 2 minutes on each side until golden brown. Remove and drain on paper towels; keep warm. Wipe out the pan.

Heat 3 tablespoons olive oil with the butter in the frying pan. Dust the liver with seasoned flour, then add to the hot pan. Fry for 2 to 3 minutes on each side, depending on thickness, until the liver is browned on the outside, but still nicely pink and juicy inside. To check whether it is ready, press the surface with your fingertips: if it feels lightly springy it's ready. If the liver feels very bouncy, it will be undercooked. Let rest for 5 minutes before serving.

At the same time, cook the fig halves: Fry these, cut-side down, in a lightly oiled pan (or alongside the liver if there is room) for 2 minutes without turning.

Place the liver on warmed plates and sprinkle with a little balsamic vinegar. Arrange the fried polenta wedges alongside and top with the hot figs. Pour the fig dressing into the pan, stirring to combine with the meat juices, then drizzle this around the liver and serve.

6 fresh figs

7 tablespoons (100 ml) Vinaigrette (page 218)

14 oz (400 g) calf's liver, in a thick slice about 2 inches (5 cm) thick

flour, for dusting

olive oil, for frying

2 tablespoons (25 g) butter

aged balsamic vinegar, for serving

sea salt and freshly ground black pepper

Polenta:

2½ cups (600 ml) milk

2½ cups (600 ml) water

2 tablespoons olive oil

1 teaspoon thyme leaves

2 cups (250 g) polenta or cornmeal (not the quick-cooking variety)

2½ tablespoons (30 g) butter

¼ cup (30 g) freshly grated Parmesan cheese

BALSAMIC VINEGAR *A few drops of balsamic vinegar provide a sharp contrast to rich meat dishes, such as meltingly soft calf's liver. Always use a brand that has been aged by the traditional method—in wooden casks for at least 10 years. Dark in color, aged balsamic vinegar has a wonderful mellow flavor.*

venison with root vegetables

THIS IS MY VERSION OF A NAVARIN. *Normally a slow-cooked casserole of lamb with potatoes and onions, I use lean venison, which I sauté and serve with a selection of winter roots, brown-butter Brussels sprouts, and a beautiful shallot, raspberry vinegar, and red wine sauce. You could call it a posh stew. Parsnip chips are the ideal accompaniment.*

SERVES 4 AS A MAIN DISH

1 ¼-lb (600-g) loin of venison

2 carrots

½ head celeriac, about 10 oz (300 g)

5 oz (150 g) baby Brussels sprouts, trimmed

3½ tablespoons (50 g) butter

6 tablespoons olive oil

sea salt and freshly ground black pepper

Sauce:

2 tablespoons olive oil

8 small or 2 large shallots, sliced

1 thyme sprig

1 bay leaf

1 fat garlic clove, sliced

750-ml bottle red wine

2 tablespoons raspberry vinegar

3½ cups (800 ml) Brown Chicken Stock (page 210)

For serving:

Parsnip Chips (page 134)

First, make the sauce: Heat the olive oil in a large saucepan, add the shallots, and sauté for about 10 minutes until softened and lightly browned. Add the thyme, bay leaf, and garlic, and sauté for a minute or two, then pour in the wine and 1 tablespoon of the vinegar. Bring to a boil, then boil rapidly until reduced to just under ½ cup (100 ml) of rich glaze.

Pour in the stock, return to a boil, and cook over a medium heat for about 20 minutes. Strain and return the liquid to the pan. Boil this down to about 1 cup (200 ml), skimming frequently to remove any scum. You should have a wonderful shiny sauce that is thick enough to lightly coat the back of a spoon. Stir in the remaining raspberry vinegar and check the seasoning. Set aside.

Cut the venison into 1½-inch (4-cm) cubes. Peel the carrots and celeriac and cut into ¾-inch (2-cm) dice. Boil the sprouts for just 2 minutes, then drain and plunge into a bowl of ice water or run cold water over them in a colander.

Heat the butter until it begins to foam. Watch carefully and, as soon as the butter stops foaming and has turned a light brown color, pour the liquid into a cup, leaving the solid particles behind. Set the liquid butter aside.

Heat 3 tablespoons olive oil in a pan and sauté the diced vegetables for about 10 minutes, stirring occasionally, until just tender. Season and remove to a plate. Keep warm, uncovered, in a low oven.

Wipe out the pan, then add the remaining olive oil and place over a medium-high heat. Sauté the venison cubes until caramelized on all sides, but still pink in the center, about 7 to 10 minutes. Season well. The venison chunks are ready if they feel lightly springy when pressed. Keep warm while you finish the sprouts.

Reheat the clarified nut-brown butter in a sauté pan. Add the sprouts and toss well to coat with the butter and heat through.

Reheat the sauce. Divide the meat and vegetables among shallow serving bowls and pour the sauce over them. Serve at once, with parsnip chips on top.

CHEF'S SECRET *Farmed venison is a wonderful lean, tender meat. Our venison comes from an estate in Scotland, where the deer roam relatively free. Before cooking we usually marinate the venison in peanut oil with crushed juniper berries and fresh rosemary or thyme for several days. This makes the meat very tender—perfect for this quick-cook stew.*

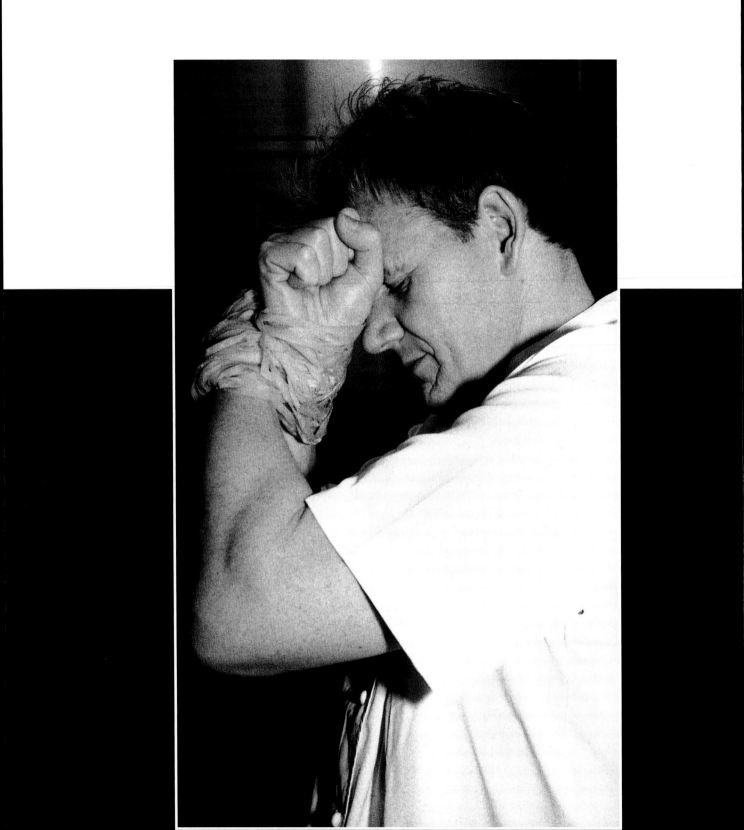

Pasta and rice

I FIRST HONED MY PASTA-MAKING SKILLS *under Marco Pierre White in the heady days of Harveys Restaurant, in London. Marco is one amazing teacher and I was an entranced follower. He taught me the meaning of fingertip control and the discipline of flexible fingers as I molded hundreds of perfect raviolis each week. I even found myself going through the motions with my hands in the early morning cab back to my small flat. I had to make sure the fillings were molded into perfectly rounded flying-saucer shapes.*

Cooked fillings called for thin pasta; raw fillings like lobster needed to be wrapped in thicker pasta. There was a pasta machine designated for each. I messed up once and put a fresh lobster filling in the wrong pasta. It all went in the bin and the cost, £45 (about $70), was deducted from my wages. It was a hard lesson, but one I never forgot. Fresh pasta dough is made twice a day in all my restaurants, and features in practically every course—including first and main courses and even sweet petit fours.

It was in the Paris kitchens of Guy Savoy where I learned the secret of blanching risotto rice grains and finishing off a risotto of shellfish with mascarpone and white truffles. I remember my time there well. As a new British commis with precious little French under my belt, I found that my inability to speak the language gave me certain advantages. For a start, I couldn't understand the oaths hurled in my direction. I just kept my head down and learned, learned, learned—everything from "turning" an artichoke to washing and drying spinach.

homemade pasta

ROLLING HOMEMADE PASTA IS REALLY A JOB FOR TWO PEOPLE—*one to crank the machine and one to tease the sheet of pasta out of the rollers and stop it folding back on itself—though, of course, it's possible to manage by yourself if there isn't anyone around to help. This basic recipe produces quite a large amount of pasta dough, because I find it easier to make a larger quantity than work with a small amount. For tagliatelle, ravioli, and tortellini, you will need about half of this quantity. You can freeze the pasta sheets that you don't need in batches for later use. Interleave them with freezer wrap and seal well, or keep well wrapped in the refrigerator for a few days. I like to use Italian pasta flour, but you can substitute all-purpose flour.*
MAKES 2 LB (900 G)

4¾ cups pasta flour or 4 cups all-
    purpose flour
¼ teaspoon sea salt
4 medium eggs
6 medium egg yolks
2 tablespoons olive oil

To make the pasta, put the flour, salt, eggs, egg yolks, and olive oil into a food processor and whiz until the mixture comes together to form coarse crumbs.

Tip this into a bowl and gather into a ball with your hands. Turn onto a lightly floured surface and knead well until the pasta dough is smooth and soft, but not sticky. Wrap in plastic wrap and let rest for 30 minutes or so.

Take a piece of dough about the size of a kiwifruit; keep the rest well wrapped to prevent it from drying out. Flatten the piece of dough to a rectangle, about ¼ inch (5 mm) thick. With the pasta machine set to its thickest setting, feed the dough through two or three times. Adjust the setting by one notch and repeat. Continue in this way, narrowing the setting by one notch each time. The dough will get progressively smoother and more elastic. When you reach the thinnest setting, the pasta is ready to be cut, filled, and shaped as required. Repeat with the remaining dough.

For ravioli or tortellini, simply cut out the required shapes from the pasta sheets. For tagliatelle, let the sheets dry for 10 minutes before cutting—drape them over the back of a clean chair, for example. Meanwhile, fit the pasta machine with the tagliatelle cutters. Pass the pasta sheet through the machine cutters, keeping the noodles separate as they emerge. When the pasta sheet has passed through the cutters, lift the noodles onto a tray, twirling them into a nest as you do so.

SAFFRON PASTA *We use saffron water to give fresh pasta an inviting rich color and subtle flavor. Our concentrated saffron essence, or saffron water (page 98) as we call it, is the secret here. Simply add a few drops to the mixture as you whiz it in the processor.*

Ravioli of confit duck with thyme velouté

I LOVE TO MAKE PASTA—*there is something so therapeutic about preparing and rolling the dough, and a pasta machine makes the task so easy. Here ravioli are filled with a delicious combination of confit duck, chicken mousse, and wild mushrooms, then served in a thyme velouté.* SERVES 4 AS A MAIN COURSE

First prepare a chicken mousse. Put the chicken breast in a small food processor or blender and whiz to a fine purée. Transfer to a bowl and fold in the cream to bind the mixture. Season generously with salt and pepper.

Melt the butter in a small pan and pan-fry the mushrooms until just soft. Place the duck meat in a bowl and mix in the mushrooms. Gradually incorporate enough chicken mousse to bind the mixture together. Add the chopped herbs and season.

Form the meat mixture into small balls, about 1 inch (2.5 cm) in diameter, and set aside.

Cut the pasta into eight pieces, roll into balls and keep wrapped in plastic wrap until ready to use. Roll out one piece of dough, using a pasta machine into a long sheet, 32 by 5 inches (80 by 12 cm), see homemade pasta (page 86). Repeat with the rest of the dough and keep the rolled sheets covered with a clean cloth.

Shape and fill the ravioli (see pages 92 to 93) and transfer to a tray lined with a clean cloth. Chill, uncovered, until required.

Bring a large pan of water to a boil, add the ravioli and cook for 2 minutes. Drain and keep warm. Meanwhile, heat the velouté until hot but not boiling. Add the ravioli and allow to warm through briefly. Serve immediately, in small bowls or on a bed of buttered cabbage.

½ cup (125 g) chopped chicken breast fillet

1 tablespoon heavy cream

1 tablespoon (25 g) unsalted butter

½ cup (50 g) wild mushrooms, finely chopped

1 quantity Duck Confit meat (page 65), shredded

1 tablespoon finely chopped chervil or chives

½ quantity Pasta Dough (page 86)

1 quantity Thyme Velouté (page 212), made with chicken stock

sea salt and freshly ground black pepper

CHEF'S TIP *For added color and flavor, try using saffron pasta (see left) for these ravioli. Alternatively, if you are very short of time, cheat and buy ready-made fresh pasta sheets from your local delicatessen or supermarket.*

tagliatelle of wild mushrooms

WILD MUSHROOMS HAVE DISTINCTIVE *individual flavors that combine beautifully in sauces. They are largely interchangeable here, so make your selection according to the season. Or you can use a mixture of wild mushrooms and cultivated mushrooms for a cheaper option. Fresh wild mushrooms usually contain grit, so they need to be washed carefully. This is a simple pasta dish, which you can embellish with a mushroom velouté for a special occasion.* SERVES 4 AS A MAIN COURSE

1 lb (450 g) fresh tagliatelle, preferably homemade (page 86, ½ quantity)
8–10 oz (250–300 g) mixed mushrooms (such as chanterelles, morels, shitake and oyster mushrooms)
2 tablespoons olive oil
1 shallot, minced
2 tablespoons (25 g) butter
½ cup (100 ml) heavy cream
4 oz (100 g) arugula or baby spinach leaves, washed
sea salt and freshly ground black pepper

For serving:
Mushroom Velouté (see right, optional)
2 oz (50 g) Parmesan cheese, finely pared into shavings

Set the tagliatelle aside while you prepare the mushrooms. Pick over the wild mushrooms and trim the ends. Slice larger ones, if necessary. Soak for a few minutes in a bowl of tepid water, swishing with your hands so all debris sinks to the bottom. Lift out the mushrooms and shake well, then pat dry in a large, clean towel or paper towels.

Heat the olive oil in a large frying pan, add the shallot, and sauté gently for 2 minutes until softened. Add the butter and, when it has melted and starts to foam, toss in the cleaned mushrooms. Sauté for about 5 minutes until they are softened. Season to taste, then mix in the cream and cook for a minute or so.

Meanwhile, cook the pasta in a large pan of boiling salted water for 1 to 2 minutes until just al dente. Drain and toss with the mushrooms, then add the arugula or spinach and heat until the leaves wilt. Check the seasoning.

Divide the mushroom pasta among warmed deep plates or large, shallow bowls and pour on the velouté, if required. Serve topped with the Parmesan shavings.

CHEF'S SECRET *Wild mushroom trimmings are full of flavor, so don't waste them. Spread them on a plate lined with paper towel and leave in a warm place for a day or until dry and crisp. Or, microwave on a low setting for 5 minutes or so, until crisp. Store in a bag for up to 1 month.*

MUSHROOM VELOUTÉ *Soak 2 oz (50 g) dried mushrooms (morels, porcini, or dried trimmings) in 1 cup (200 ml) boiling water for about 10 minutes, then lift out and chop. Strain the liquid through a fine sieve and reserve. Gently sauté 1 minced shallot in 2 tablespoons olive oil until softened but not colored. Add the mushrooms and ½ cup (150 ml) dry white wine. Simmer until reduced by half, then pour in the mushroom liquid and 1¼ cups (300 ml) Brown Chicken Stock (page 210). Bring to a boil and simmer until reduced by half again. Finally, stir in ½ cup (100 ml) heavy cream, return to a simmer, and cook for about 5 minutes. Strain the sauce through a sieve into a cup, pressing with the back of a ladle. Reheat to serve.*

CHEF'S SECRET *Typically, pasta is tossed with sage leaves that have been fried in butter until frazzled and crisp. My way of serving pasta—in a sage-infused, cream-enriched beurre noisette with shredded fresh sage leaves added at the last moment—gives an altogether different result. None of the fragrance or fresh flavor of the sage is lost.*

pumpkin and amaretti ravioli

THIS RAVIOLI RECIPE COMES FROM ANGELA HARNETT *at The Connaught. It is one that she acquired from her Italian grandmother. Adding a small handful of crushed amaretti to a pumpkin ravioli filling is an Italian custom—it adds a light texture and a hint of sweet almond flavor. I like to serve the ravioli tossed in a sage-infused beurre noisette with shreds of fresh sage, butter, and shavings of Parmesan. You will need to cook the pumpkin a day in advance. Be sure to use a piece from a small pumpkin. Or you could substitute butternut squash.* SERVES 6–8 AS A MAIN COURSE

Preheat the oven to 350°F (180°C). Remove seeds and fibers from the pumpkin, then peel and chop. Mix with 4 tablespoons olive oil and place on a large sheet of foil. Season and draw the foil up over the pumpkin. Place the foil parcel on a baking sheet and bake for up to 1 hour until soft. Cool slightly, then whiz in a food processor until smooth. Spoon into a large strainer set over a bowl. Let cool, then refrigerate overnight to allow excess liquid to drain away.

The next day, tip the drained pumpkin into a bowl. Finely grate half of the Parmesan. Sauté the shallots in the remaining olive oil for 5 minutes to soften, then mix into the pumpkin along with the bread crumbs, grated Parmesan, and seasoning. Crush 3 of the amaretti and mix these in too. Set aside.

Cut the pasta into eight pieces and roll into balls; keep wrapped until ready to roll. Using a pasta machine, roll each pasta ball into a long sheet, about 32 by 5 inches (80 by 13 cm)—see Homemade Pasta, page 86. Repeat with the rest. Keep covered with a clean towel.

Shape the ravioli (see pages 92 to 93) and place on a tray lined with a clean towel. Chill, uncovered, until ready to serve. Pare the remaining piece of Parmesan into fine shavings. Crush the last of the amaretti and set aside.

To make the sage beurre noisette, strip the leaves from the sage stems and set aside. Put the unsalted butter in a saucepan with the sage stems and melt slowly, then increase the heat and cook until the moment the butter starts to turn brown. Immediately take off the heat and let stand for 1 minute. Slowly strain the butter through a fine sieve into a clean pan, leaving the sediment behind. Discard the sage stems. Shred the sage leaves as finely as you can. Return the beurre noisette to a low heat and stir in the cream, then take off the heat and add the shredded sage leaves.

Meanwhile, bring a large pan of lightly salted water to a boil, add the ravioli, and cook for 2 minutes. Drain and return to the pan. Add the sage beurre noisette and seasoning, and toss gently to mix.

Serve in warmed shallow bowls, with the last of the crushed amaretti and Parmesan shavings scattered on top.

1 quantity homemade Saffron Pasta Dough (page 86)
1 large egg yolk, beaten with 1 teaspoon cold water

Filling and for serving:

3½-lb (1.5-kg) piece of pumpkin
6 tablespoons olive oil
5 oz (150 g) Parmesan cheese
2 large shallots, chopped
2 cups (100 g) fresh white bread crumbs
4 amaretti cookies
sea salt and freshly ground black pepper

Sage beurre noisette:

6 sage sprigs, plus stems
5 tablespoons (75 g) unsalted butter, in pieces
2 tablespoons heavy cream

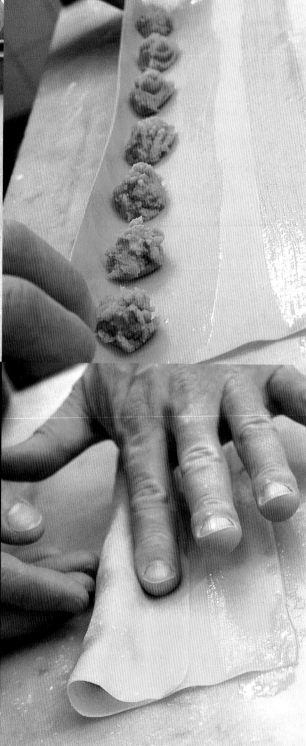

TO SHAPE RAVIOLI *Lay one pasta sheet on a clean surface and trim the edges to neaten. With a long edge near you, place teaspoonfuls of filling along one-third of the pasta, spacing them about ½ inch (1 cm) apart. Brush the pasta around the filling with egg wash; lightly brush the other two-thirds of the dough too. Carefully fold the pumpkin-topped third of the pasta over, to enclose the filling, and press the pasta around it to seal and exclude any air gaps. Fold the other third of the pasta over the top and press between the filling with your fingers. Using a fluted pasta cutter, cut between the filling mounds to make the ravioli. Repeat with the remaining pasta sheets and filling.*

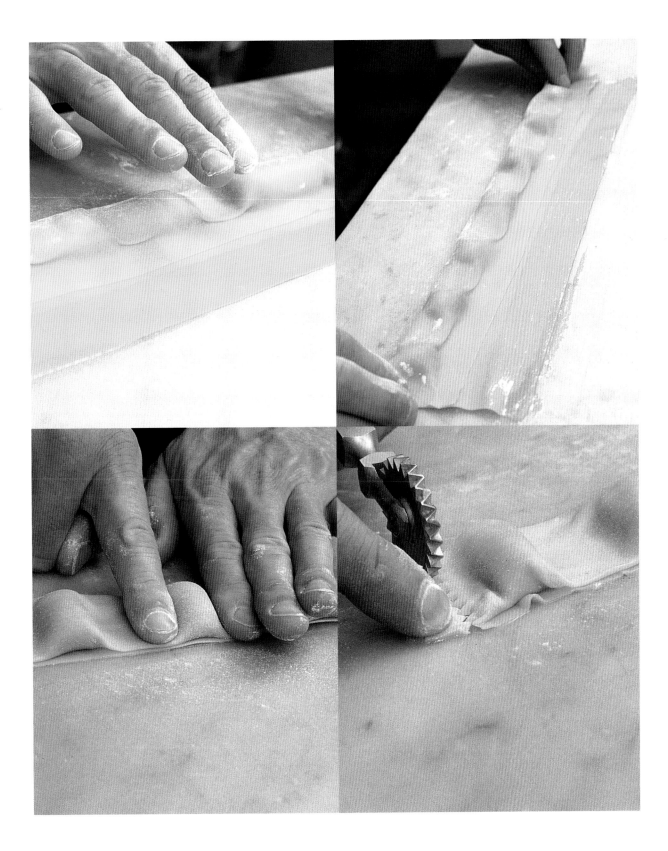

smoked haddock and asparagus open ravioli

FRESH PASTA ROUNDS ARE LAYERED *with a light, creamy sauce of smoked haddock and asparagus tips, then served topped with lightly poached quail eggs, for a new take on lasagne. Serve simply as an elegant lunch, or make a delicate asparagus velouté with the trimmings and spoon around the pasta ensemble for a special occasion.* SERVES 4 AS A FIRST COURSE OR LIGHT MEAL

Using a 3-inch (7- to 8-cm) plain cutter, cut out 12 rounds from the pasta sheets, then cover and set aside until ready to cook.

Poach the smoked haddock fillet in the milk for 5 to 7 minutes until the flesh is just beginning to flake. Remove the fish from the milk and leave until cool enough to handle, then skin and flake the flesh.

Cut the stalks from the asparagus spears, leaving about 4-inch (10-cm) tips. Reserve the asparagus stalks for the velouté. Blanch the tips in salted water for 1 to 2 minutes until just tender, then drain and plunge into a bowl of ice water to refresh.

Put the crème fraîche into a small pan and heat gently, then add the flaked haddock, asparagus tips, and chives. Heat through. Check the seasoning.

Meanwhile, cook the pasta in a pan of boiling water for 1 to 2 minutes until al dente, then drain and toss with the melted butter. At the same time, if using quail eggs, cook them in a small pan of boiling water for 1 to 1½ minutes until lightly cooked. Drain and shell, then carefully coat with a little of the creamy sauce base.

To assemble, place a round of pasta on each warmed plate. Add a layer of the asparagus and haddock sauce, then another pasta round. Repeat these layers, then top with the quail eggs and spoon a little more sauce over them. Serve with asparagus velouté, if desired.

about 8 oz (225 g) fresh pasta sheets, preferably homemade (page 86, ¼ quantity)

Filling:
1 large fillet of smoked haddock, about 14 oz (400 g)
2 cups (500 ml) milk
10 oz (300 g) thin asparagus spears
7 fl oz (200 ml) crème fraîche
1 tablespoon chopped chives
2 tablespoons (25 g) butter, melted
12 quail eggs (optional)
sea salt and freshly ground black pepper

For serving:
Asparagus Velouté (see right, optional)

ASPARAGUS VELOUTÉ *Mince the reserved asparagus stalks and sauté with 1 minced large shallot in 2 tablespoons olive oil for about 5 minutes until softened. Add a handful baby spinach leaves and the chopped leaves from a sprig of tarragon. Cook until wilted, then pour in 1¼ cups (300 ml) Fish Stock (page 209). Bring to a boil, lower the heat, and simmer for 10 minutes. Whiz in a blender or food processor, then pass through a strainer, rubbing with the back of a ladle. Return the sauce to the pan and stir in 2 tablespoons heavy cream. Reheat gently to serve.*

spaetzle

THIS IS THE GERMAN ANSWER TO PASTA, *but it's easier to prepare. You simply make a thick eggy batter, then rub it through a special sieve or colander directly into a pan of boiling water and the batter sets instantly into soft doughy squiggles. Once they are cooked and drained, I fry the spaetzle in beurre noisette so they puff up, become crisp, and turn golden brown. Serve as an accompaniment to rich meat and game stews, or with a light tomato sauce and freshly grated Parmesan for a light meal.*
SERVES 4–6 AS AN ACCOMPANIMENT OR LIGHT MEAL

Sift the flour and salt together into a large bowl. Gradually beat in the eggs, then the water, until you have a batter with a thick but pourable consistency. If necessary, add a little extra water. Let rest for 2 hours. In the meantime, make the beurre noisette (see below).

When ready to cook, bring a large pan of water to a boil. Have ready a large bowl of ice water. Place a spaetzle sieve or colander over the pan of boiling water.

You will need to cook the spaetzle in batches. Ladle some runny dough onto the sieve and immediately rub through, using a dough scraper or the back of the ladle. As soon as the dough is through, remove the sieve. When they are just cooked, the spaetzle will rise to the surface. Allow them a few more seconds, then lift out with a slotted spoon into the bowl of ice water. Repeat in batches until the dough is used up. Drain and dry on paper towels.

Fry the spaetzle in two batches: Heat one-quarter of the beurre noisette in a large frying pan, add half the spaetzle, and fry until lightly browned. Add another quarter of the butter and continue to fry until the spaetzle are puffed up and crisp. Season generously with salt, pepper, and nutmeg. Drain on paper towels and keep warm while you fry the rest. Serve hot, sprinkled with minced herbs.

1⅔ cups (250 g) all-purpose flour
1 teaspoon fine sea salt
4 large eggs, beaten
about 3 tablespoons cold water
Beurre Noisette (see below)
freshly grated nutmeg, to taste
sea salt and freshly ground black pepper
minced herbs (parsley, basil, or chervil),
  for serving

BEURRE NOISETTE *Slowly heat ½ cup (125 g) unsalted butter in a saucepan, then increase the heat and cook until the moment the butter starts to turn brown. Immediately take the pan off the heat and let stand for 1 minute. Then slowly pour the golden brown butter into a bowl, leaving the sediment behind in the pan.*

my saffron shellfish risotto

PREPARING A CLASSIC, CREAMY RISOTTO *by the traditional method can take up to 20 minutes with constant attention, and this isn't a dish you can prepare ahead and reheat successfully. We don't test our clients' patience in the restaurant, and neither need you keep your guests waiting at home if you adopt my risotto technique (described below and illustrated on page 100). It halves the cooking time. Of the different varieties of risotto rice available, my personal favorite is Carnaroli because the grains are plump and remain firm.* SERVES 4 AS A FIRST COURSE OR LIGHT MEAL

scant 1 cup (200 g) risotto rice
(Carnaroli, Arborio, or Vialone Nano)
20 langoustines (lobsterettes), or
7 oz (200 g) raw tiger shrimp (heads removed)
⅔ cup (100 g) shelled fresh baby fava beans
about 2 cups (500 ml) Chicken Stock (page 210) or Fish Stock (page 209)
3 tablespoons olive oil
1 large or 3 smaller shallots, minced
4 tablespoons dry white wine
3½ tablespoons (50 g) butter, chilled and cubed
1 teaspoon saffron water (see below)
1 tablespoon minced chervil
1 tablespoon minced chives
2 tablespoons freshly grated Parmesan cheese
sea salt and freshly ground black pepper
Parmesan cheese shavings, for serving

Bring a large pan of salted water to a boil. Add the risotto rice and blanch for 5 minutes, then drain and spread out on a tray. Cover and set aside until ready to cook, or chill if you are several hours ahead of serving.

Prepare the langoustines (see page 20); if using shrimp, peel and devein. Set the peeled langoustines or shrimp aside.

Blanch the baby fava beans in boiling water for 2 to 3 minutes, then drain and slip the beans out of their skins. Season and set aside.

Bring the stock to a simmer in a pan. Meanwhile, heat the olive oil in a larger pan and sauté the shallot for 3 minutes until softened. Stir in the rice and cook for about 2 minutes, stirring frequently. Add the wine and reduce right down.

Now add one-third of the stock and stir frequently until the stock is almost all absorbed. Add another third of the stock, and stir until absorbed. Add half of the remaining stock, then add the fava beans and stir gently. Once this stock is absorbed, check the rice grains. If they are still a little chalky, then add more stock. (This stage only takes around 10 minutes.)

In the meantime, heat half the butter in a frying pan until it starts to foam. Add the langoustines or shrimp and stir-fry until bright pink and firm, about 3 minutes. Season and set aside.

When the risotto is creamy and the rice is al dente (cooked, but retaining a bite), stir in the saffron water, followed by the herbs and Parmesan. Finally, stir in the remaining butter and check the seasoning.

Divide the risotto among warmed bowls. Arrange the langoustines or tiger shrimp on top and scatter on some Parmesan shavings. Serve immediately.

SAFFRON WATER *We buy Spanish saffron and make a concentrated essence by crushing saffron strands into a little boiling water. The infused "saffron water" gives risottos and pasta dishes an exotic flavor and rich color. To make this, mix 1 teaspoon of saffron strands with 3 to 4 tablespoons boiling water, then cool. Keep in a jar in the refrigerator for up to 3 days, or freeze as tiny ice cubes.*

THE PERFECT RISOTTO *Heat the oil in a medium, heavy-based pan and sauté the shallot for 3 minutes until softened, then stir in the rice and cook for about 2 minutes, stirring frequently. Add the wine and reduce right down.*

Now add one-third of the stock and stir frequently until the stock is almost all absorbed. Add another third of the stock, and stir until absorbed.

Add half of the remaining stock, then add the fava beans and stir gently. Once this stock is absorbed, check the rice grains. If they are still a little chalky, then add more stock. (This stage only takes around 10 minutes.)

When the risotto is creamy and the rice is al dente (cooked, but retaining a bite), stir in the saffron water, followed by the herbs and Parmesan. Finally, stir in the remaining butter in cubes.

herb risotto with sautéed scallops

BEING DELICIOUSLY SWEET AND CREAMY, *scallops can be paired with a wide variety of different flavorings, from Asian and spicy to rich red wines. Sautéed scallops are delicious served simply with a green salad, but I also like to serve them with a freshly cooked herb risotto. Full-bodied Barolo, one of the great wines of Italy, is reduced down with port to make a rich glaze for the scallops.* SERVES 4 AS A FIRST COURSE OR 2 AS A MAIN DISH

1 cup (250 ml) Barolo wine

1 cup (250 ml) ruby port

2½ cups (600 ml) Chicken Stock (page 210) or Fish Stock (page 209)

about 4 tablespoons olive oil

1 shallot, minced

scant 1 cup (200 g) risotto rice (Carnaroli, Arborio, or Vialone Nano)

4 tablespoons dry white wine

6 sea scallops, cleaned (see page 19)

1 tablespoon (15 g) butter

1 tablespoon chopped tarragon

1 tablespoon chopped basil

1 tablespoon chopped chives

sea salt and freshly ground black pepper

extra chopped herbs, for serving

First, make your reduction: Pour the Barolo and port into a saucepan and bring to a boil. Bubble until reduced to about 4 tablespoons, to make a syrupy glaze. Set aside to cool.

To make the risotto, bring the stock to a simmer in a saucepan. Meanwhile, heat 2 tablespoons olive oil in a deep saucepan and sauté the shallot for about 5 minutes until softened. Add the rice and cook for 2 minutes until the grains are opaque. Pour in the white wine and cook until reduced right down.

Add one-fourth of the simmering stock and cook, stirring, until it is all absorbed. Add the remaining stock, a ladleful at a time, making sure each addition is absorbed before adding another. This should take about 15 minutes, by which time the rice will be tender but still have a good bite. You may not need to add all of the stock. Season with salt and pepper to taste.

When the risotto is almost cooked, heat a heavy-based frying pan or ridged grill pan until you feel a good heat rising. Add a thin film of olive oil, then place the scallops in the pan, in a circle. Cook for 1½ minutes, then turn (in the same order you placed them in the pan to ensure even cooking). Cook the other side for a minute or so, until golden. Press the scallops with the back of a fork: if they feel slightly springy they are ready. Remove to a warmed plate and let rest while you finish the risotto.

Stir the butter and chopped herbs into the risotto. Warm the red wine and port glaze. Slice each scallop in half horizontally. Spoon the risotto into shallow bowls, arrange the scallops on top, and trickle the glaze over them. Drizzle with a little olive oil and sprinkle with extra chopped herbs. Serve immediately.

wild rice jambalaya

I LOVE THE CAJUN INSPIRATION OF THIS LOUISIANA DISH, *a total meal created in one pot—just as it would have been prepared in the Bayou, with all the local ingredients to hand.* SERVES 4

Combine all the herbs, spices, and seasonings in a small bowl and set aside.

Melt the margarine in a large, heavy skillet. Add the smoked ham and sausage, and cook for 5 minutes, stirring occasionally.

Add the onions, celery, bell peppers, and garlic, and cook for a further 10 minutes, stirring from time to time.

Add the rice and cook for 5 minutes, stirring to coat all the grains in the fat. Pour in the stock, bring to a boil, then lower the heat and simmer for 20 minutes or until the rice is cooked.

Sprinkle with the chopped cilantro and serve immediately.

4 small bay leaves

1 thyme sprig, leaves only

½ teaspoon ground cumin

1 teaspoon cayenne pepper

½ teaspoon freshly ground black pepper

1 teaspoon yellow mustard seeds

1 teaspoon dry mustard

1 teaspoon gumbo file (optional)

1 teaspoon salt

4 tablespoons margarine

6 oz (175 g) smoked ham (such as tasso), chopped

6 oz (175 g) smoked sausage (such as keilbassa), chopped

1½ cups (175 g) chopped onions

1½ cups (175 g) chopped celery

1 cup (175 g) chopped bell peppers

2 garlic cloves, minced

2 cups (500 g) easy-cook mixed long-grain and wild rice

4 cups (1 liter) Chicken Stock (page 210)

4 tablespoons cilantro, finely chopped

VEGETABLES

THE PASSPORT OF MY MENUS *is the seasonality of vegetables, not fish or meat. Of course, it's now possible to ignore the seasons and buy in the same vegetables all year round, but the ethics, flavor, and diversity of seasonal vegetables makes for a far more interesting menu.*

I focus hard on homegrown produce, perhaps fueled by my childhood experiences. School vacations were often spent picking vegetables for money. Our home in Shipston-on-Stour was close to the market gardens in the Vale of Evesham. I associate early spring with cutting green asparagus stems, not for our own use but for the growers to bunch and sell on. We lunched on fresh asparagus soup made, no doubt, from trimmings, so I grew up with a taste for it.

As a teen-ager I was passionate about fishing, but times were not easy for us as a family then. Bank holiday weekends coincided with the potato harvest, so we would go camping to Broadstairs in Kent, and pick potatoes for money. I found that if I fixed sacks between my legs and shoveled in spuds as fast as I could on the Saturday, I could earn enough in a day to spend Sunday fishing off Margate Pier.

As a consequence of my youth, I have learned to hate waste. How stupid to turn potatoes into silly barrel shapes and waste good flesh. Why throw asparagus trimmings away when they can be turned into amazing soup? I love to feel fresh spears between my fingers as I consider how to cook them. The short intimate season of white asparagus is, to my mind, on a par with the fleeting appearance of white truffle.

watercress and potato soup

THIS IS ONE OF THOSE INVALUABLE RECIPES *that can be built on and taken to new heights each time you make it. At its simplest, it is a fresh tasting, velvety-smooth soup that's delicious served hot, topped with a dollop of crème fraîche. Or, you can serve it chilled as a refreshing summer soup, infused with olive-oil ice cubes, if desired—to keep it cool and impart flavor as they slowly melt. For a special occasion, float a poached egg in the center of each serving and top with a spoonful of caviar (as illustrated)—you break the softly set egg into the soup as you eat it. Or, if you prefer, simply garnish each portion with a poached oyster.*
SERVES 2 AS A FIRST COURSE

4 cups (1 liter) Vegetable Nage
   (page 211)
1 vegetable bouillon cube
2 tablespoons olive oil
1 large shallot, minced
1½ cups (200 g) peeled and finely
   diced waxy boiling potatoes
8 oz (250 g) watercress, well washed
small handful of baby spinach leaves
sea salt and freshly ground black
   pepper

For serving:
either 2 tablespoons crème fraîche,
   lightly whipped, or 4 large poached
   eggs (see page 140) and 1-oz (25-g)
   can caviar, or 4 poached oysters
olive oil, for drizzling

For the stock, bring the vegetable nage to a boil, crumble in the bouillon cube, and stir until dissolved.

Heat the olive oil in a large saucepan and gently sauté the shallot and potatoes for 5 to 7 minutes until softened. Do not let them color.

Pour in the vegetable stock and bring to a rolling boil, then drop in the watercress and spinach. As soon as the leaves wilt, remove the pan from the heat and transfer the leaves and potato to a food processor, using a slotted spoon; reserve the stock.

Whiz the mixture until smooth, adding the stock gradually. This is best done in stages to ensure a very smooth texture. Chill until required (unless you are serving the soup hot and straight away).

To serve hot, reheat the soup (if necessary). For a simple finish, ladle into warmed bowls and top with a dollop of crème fraîche. For a more elaborate finish, slide a poached egg into each bowl and top with a spoonful of caviar. Alternatively, float a poached oyster on each serving.

To serve chilled, divide the soup among chilled bowls, drizzle with a little olive oil, and add a few olive-oil ice cubes to each serving, if desired.

INFUSED ICE CUBES *Use 2 cups (500 ml) of Vegetable Nage (page 211). Pour three-fourths into icecube trays, to fill about 20 cavities. Freeze until solid around the edge, but still partially liquid in the center. Using the tip of a small teaspoon, hollow out the center of each cube and pour in about 1 teaspoon olive oil. Carefully pour in a little more stock to cover, then freeze until solid. The oil should be trapped inside each ice cube, like a bubble. Use straight from the freezer.*

CHEF'S SECRET *If I am serving this soup warm, topped with poached eggs, I find it less of a hassle to prepare the eggs in advance. Follow the instructions for poaching eggs on page 140. When ready to serve, simply place a poached egg in each bowl—the heat of the soup will be sufficient to warm the eggs through.*

asparagus soup with truffle cream

MAKE THIS SOUP IN THE SPRING *when homegrown asparagus is in season and available at a good price. You don't need to seek out young, tender spears—it's the flavor you need, not the texture. You will achieve a good result with a combination of stalks and trimmings, so don't discard the woody ends and peelings if you're preparing asparagus to serve as a vegetable—use them here. Adding a couple of handfuls of tender spinach leaves helps to boost the natural asparagus color without detracting from the flavor.*
SERVES 4 AS A FIRST COURSE

2¼ lb (1 kg) green asparagus
   (including trimmings, if available)
5 tablespoons (75 g) butter
1 onion, chopped
1 fat garlic clove, chopped
3 cups (750 ml) Chicken Stock
   (page 210) or Vegetable Nage
   (page 211)
4 oz (100 g) baby leaf spinach
sea salt and freshly ground black pepper

For serving:
⅔ cup (150 ml) heavy cream
½ teaspoon truffle oil
2 teaspoons minced chives

Chop the asparagus into small, even-sized pieces. Heat the butter in a large saucepan and, when it starts to sizzle, add the onion and garlic. Sauté gently for about 10 minutes until softened but not colored. Add the asparagus pieces and sauté for 5 to 10 minutes, until softened.

Meanwhile, bring the chicken stock or vegetable nage to a boil in another pan.

Pour the hot stock over the asparagus, season to taste, and simmer for 3 minutes. Then stir in the spinach and cook briefly, until just wilted. Immediately remove from the heat and drain the vegetables, reserving the stock.

Purée the vegetables in a blender or food processor, gradually adding the stock until you have a creamy liquid. Strain the soup through a sieve into a clean pan (or bowl if you are not serving straight away; see below). Rub the pulp in the sieve with the back of a ladle to extract as much flavor as possible.

To serve, lightly whip the cream with the truffle oil and seasoning until softly peaking. Reheat the soup gently until almost at a simmer, but do not boil or you will destroy the amazing color and flavor. Serve in warmed bowls topped with dollops of truffle cream and chopped chives.

CHEF'S SECRET *In the restaurant we prepare this soup ahead, as you probably will if you're entertaining. The trick is to capture the freshness and color of the asparagus. To achieve this, we cool the puréed soup as quickly as possible, by pouring it straight from the blender into a bowl that is set in a larger bowl containing plenty of ice cubes and a little water. When the soup is cold, remove from the ice water, cover, and chill until required.*

my roasted tomato soup

A SUPERLATIVE FRESH TOMATO SOUP *is one of the hallmarks of a good cook. My secret is to first roast the tomatoes, together with onions and herbs. Flavorful tomatoes are, of course, essential. To enhance the flavor I add smoked, sun-dried cherry tomatoes, which have a hickory-smoke flavor. If you can't find these, substitute snipped soft, sun-dried tomatoes and a dash of barbecue sauce. (Illustrated on page 111)*
SERVES 4 AS A FIRST COURSE

Preheat the oven to 425°F (220°C). Pour the olive oil into a roasting pan and heat in the oven until almost smoking. Carefully tip in the tomatoes, onion rings, and garlic, and toss to coat with the oil. Scatter on the thyme sprigs, sprinkle with sugar, and season generously with salt and pepper. Roast for 20 to 25 minutes until nicely caramelized, stirring once or twice and adding the basil toward the end of the cooking time.

Tip the roasted tomatoes and flavorings into a saucepan, discarding any woody thyme stems. Bring the stock to a boil in another pan, then pour it over the tomatoes. Bring to a boil, add the smoked tomatoes (or semi-soft sun-dried tomatoes plus barbecue sauce), and cook for 5 minutes.

Drain the tomato mixture, reserving the stock. Tip the tomatoes into a blender or food processor and whiz, gradually adding the stock, until smooth and creamy. Strain the soup through a sieve into a clean pan or bowl, rubbing with the back of a ladle. Taste and adjust the seasoning.

For the garnish, heat the olive oil in a frying pan. Snip the vine tomatoes into four clusters and pan-fry them, on the vine, for about 1 minute.

Reheat the soup, if necessary: it's best served warm rather than piping hot. Pour into warmed bowls and top with the pan-roasted vine tomatoes. Drizzle the pan juices around the tomatoes and scatter on some basil leaves.

4 tablespoons olive oil
2¼ lb (1 kg) plum tomatoes, halved
1 onion, thinly sliced
2 fat garlic cloves, halved
small handful of thyme sprigs
1 teaspoon sugar
small handful of basil sprigs
4 cups (1 liter) Chicken Stock
 (page 210) or Vegetable Nage
 (page 211)
3 smoked, sun-dried cherry tomatoes
 in oil, drained (or 2 semi-soft
 sun-dried tomatoes and 1 tablespoon
 barbecue sauce)
sea salt and freshly ground black pepper

For serving:
2 tablespoons olive oil
7–10 oz (200–300 g) baby cherry
 tomatoes on the vine
small basil leaves

CHEF'S TIP *For a really velvety texture, use a blender rather than a food processor to purée a creamed soup. To ensure a perfectly smooth result, pass the puréed soup through a sieve.*

warm pumpkin salad with ricotta toasts

PUMPKINS ARE IN SEASON DURING THE AUTUMN *and, of course, they are everywhere around Halloween. Pumpkin flesh has a delectable sweet, creamy flavor that lends itself beautifully to tasty soups, fillings for ravioli (see page 91), and pureés to accompany rich meats and game. Chopped and pan-roasted, it forms the basis of a fabulous first-course salad. I prefer the brown-skinned, ridged pumpkins that are popular in France and the West Indies. These are often sold in London, in thick wedges, but you can use a small, round pumpkin instead. Pumpkin oil is available from wholefood markets. Dark golden in color, with a warm, nutty aroma, it makes a tasty addition to salad dressings and is ideal for trickling over warm vegetables.*

SERVES 4 AS A FIRST COURSE

1 small, ripe pumpkin, about 2¼ lb
   (1 kg), or a piece of this weight
about 5 oz (150 g) mixed sharp salad
   leaves, such as curly endive and
   arugula
4–5 tablespoons olive oil, plus extra for
   brushing
3½ tablespoons (50 g) butter
½ small ciabatta loaf or baguette
4 tablespoons Vinaigrette (page 218)
4 tablespoons pumpkin seeds, toasted
3–5 tablespoons ricotta cheese
2 tablespoons balsamic vinegar
1 tablespoon pumpkin oil
sea salt and freshly ground black pepper
about 1 oz (25 g) Parmesan cheese,
   finely pared into shavings,
   for garnish

First, peel the pumpkin. The easiest way to do this is to cut it into wedges with a heavy-bladed knife. Scoop out the seeds and fibers, then peel off the skin, using a short, sharp knife. Chop the flesh into ½-inch (1-cm) cubes and season with salt and pepper.

Separate the endive leaves, then tear into smaller pieces. Wash the endive and arugula, dry well, and place in a large bowl. Preheat the broiler.

Heat the olive oil in a large frying pan, add the pumpkin cubes, and sauté for about 5 minutes. Add the butter and cook, shaking the pan constantly, for 3 to 4 minutes, until the pumpkin cubes are nicely caramelized and softened. Remove and drain on paper towels. Let cool slightly.

Meanwhile, slice the ciabatta or baguette thinly and brush with olive oil. Lightly toast under the broiler until crisp on both sides.

Lightly dress the salad leaves with the vinaigrette. Add the warm pumpkin cubes, pumpkin seeds, and seasoning to taste, and toss gently to mix. Divide among serving plates. Spread the ciabatta toasts with the ricotta, season, and place alongside the salad. Drizzle the balsamic vinegar and pumpkin oil over the salad and scatter on some Parmesan shavings.

CHEF'S TIP *For optimum flavor it's important to use a really ripe pumpkin here—bright golden-orange flesh indicates that the vegetable is ripe and ready to cook. Roasting, in a pan or the oven, gives a firmer texture and more pronounced flavor than boiling pumpkin.*

herb gnocchi with tomato salsa

THIS RECIPE IS ALL ABOUT *getting extra flavor into a simple dish. Rather than boil and mash potatoes in the usual way for gnocchi, I bake them for a fuller flavor and fluffier texture, then mash. Sautéeing the gnocchi in oil and butter before serving crisps the surface and gives them a delicious flavor.* SERVES 2 AS A MAIN COURSE, 4 AS A LIGHT MEAL OR FIRST COURSE

2 large baking potatoes, about
   14 oz (400 g) each

1 heaped cup (160 g) all-purpose flour

1 teaspoon fine sea salt

1 tablespoon chopped basil

1 tablespoon chopped parsley

1 extra large egg, beaten

4 tablespoons olive oil, plus extra for
   drizzling

3½ tablespoons (50 g) butter

Tomato salsa:

6 vine-ripened plum tomatoes

1 small red onion, minced

2 scallions, finely sliced

juice of 1 lime

1 tablespoon roasted sesame oil

generous dash of hot pepper sauce

1 tablespoon minced basil

1 tablespoon minced cilantro

sea salt and freshly ground black pepper

Preheat the oven to 350°F (180°C). Scrub the potatoes, but don't score or pierce them. Bake for about 1¼ hours until soft in the center when tested with a skewer. Set aside to cool for 10 minutes, then peel off the skins. Mash the potato flesh in a bowl or press through a potato ricer, then let cool completely.

When the mash is cool, mix in the flour and salt until evenly incorporated, then add the herbs. Gradually work in the beaten egg until you have a smooth, firm dough—you may not need to add all of the egg.

Bring a large pan of salted water to a boil. Have ready a large bowl of ice water. Divide the dough into eight balls. Roll out each one on a lightly floured surface to a narrow sausage about 12 inches (30 cm) long. Flatten very slightly to make an oval shape. Cut across, slightly on the diagonal, into 1¼-inch (3-cm) lengths, using the back of a table knife or thick cook's knife.

Cook the gnocchi in batches: Add about one-fourth of them to the boiling water and cook for 2 to 3 minutes, until they rise to the surface. Lift out with a slotted spoon and place in the bowl of ice water. Leave for a minute or so, then drain well on paper towels, patting them dry. Repeat to cook the remaining gnocchi, always returning the water to a rolling boil in between the batches.

When all the gnocchi have been cooked and cooled, combine them in a bowl. Drizzle with a little olive oil to keep them separate, then cover with plastic wrap and chill until required.

To make the salsa, dip the tomatoes in boiling water for 30 seconds or so to loosen the skins, then into cold water to refresh; drain and peel away the skins. Quarter the tomatoes, then remove core and seeds. Finely dice the flesh and place in a bowl with the other salsa ingredients. Toss to mix and season well, then spoon into a serving dish.

When ready to serve, heat 2 tablespoons olive oil and half the butter in a large frying pan until hot. Sauté the gnocchi, in batches, for 3 to 4 minutes until golden brown and crisp on both sides. Drain on paper towels. Keep each batch warm, uncovered, in a low oven, while you sauté the rest, using the remaining oil and butter as needed. Serve with the tomato salsa.

CHEF'S SECRET *Cutting the dough with the thicker edge of a knife has the effect of blunting the ends and gives the gnocchi their characteristic pinched edges. Cook the gnocchi as soon as you have cut them, so they don't dry out.*

tourte of field mushrooms

THESE IMPRESSIVE TOURTES *are an ideal main course if you are entertaining vegetarians. You will need to buy 12 large, open mushrooms—portobello mushrooms are ideal. Serve with a leafy salad.* SERVES 4 AS A MAIN COURSE

First, make the crêpe batter: Whiz the flour, salt, egg, and milk in a blender or food processor until smooth. Pour into a cup and let rest in the refrigerator.

Preheat the oven to 375°F (190°C). To prepare the mushrooms, wipe clean with a damp cloth, but don't wash or peel them. Cut off the stems (save for the duxelles, if desired). Brush the tops with the melted butter and place, cap-side up, in a roasting pan. Season with salt and pepper and bake for 10 minutes. Let cool in the pan, then drain off any juices and chill.

Meanwhile, prepare the mushroom duxelles: Mince the mushrooms very finely—by hand or by pulsing in a food processor. Heat the butter and oil in a frying pan until really hot, then add the mushrooms and stir-fry over a high heat until softened. Season to taste, and add the tarragon and sherry or Madeira. The duxelles should be soft, but quite dry (if necessary cook for a little longer to evaporate any liquid). Cool, then mix in the bread crumbs and egg yolk.

Stir the melted butter into the crêpe batter. Heat a 6-inch (15-cm) crêpe pan and oil lightly. Cook the crêpes, making them as thin and lacy as possible—you should make 10 to 12. Set aside the four thinnest crêpes to cool (freeze the rest).

Now, layer the whole baked mushrooms and duxelles: Trim the baked mushrooms to the same size, using a 2¾-inch (7-cm) cutter, if necessary. Spoon half the duxelles on top of 4 mushrooms. Cover each with another mushroom, then add another layer of duxelles. Finally, top with the remaining mushrooms.

Wrap each mushroom "sandwich" in a crêpe (they won't be completely enclosed). Place join-side down on a plate and refrigerate.

Set the oven to 400°F (200°C). Roll out the pastry (half at a time for easy handling) on a lightly floured board to a ⅛-inch (3-mm) thickness. Cut out four 5-inch (12-cm) rounds and four 6-inch (15-cm) rounds. Brush around the edges with egg wash. Put the mushroom crêpe parcels on the smaller rounds and cover with the larger ones. Cup one parcel upside-down in your hand and carefully press the edges together, then trim to leave a ½-inch (1-cm) edge. Crimp this with a fork. Repeat to shape the rest of the tourtes.

Place the tourtes flat-side down on a nonstick baking sheet. Score the pastry with the tip of a knife, radiating from the center, but don't cut right through. Brush all over with egg wash and let rest in the refrigerator for 15 minutes or so.

Bake the tourtes for 20 minutes or until puffed and golden brown. Leave on the baking sheet for 10 minutes, then carefully slide onto plates.

12 portobello mushrooms, at least
   3¼ inches (8 cm) in diameter
4 tablespoons (60 g) butter, melted
olive oil, for frying
1 lb (500 g) puff pastry, homemade
   (page 184) or bought
1 large egg yolk, beaten with
   1 teaspoon cold water (egg wash),
   for glazing
sea salt and freshly ground black pepper

Crêpe batter:
⅔ cup (100 g) all-purpose flour
pinch of salt
1 large egg
1 cup (250 ml) milk
1 tablespoon (15 g) butter, melted

Mushroom duxelles:
5 oz (150 g) crimini mushrooms, or wild
   mushrooms
3½ tablespoons (50 g) butter
1 tablespoon olive oil
1 teaspoon chopped tarragon
1 tablespoon sherry or Madeira
⅔ cup (30 g) fresh white bread crumbs
1 large egg yolk

assiette de legumes

VEGETARIAN DISHES ARE AN INCREASINGLY POPULAR CHOICE *in my restaurants and I enjoy creating new medleys of vegetables that enhance their fabulous colors and flavors. This simple, but sophisticated selection of vegetables is served with a light thyme velouté. Vary the vegetables according to the season and personal preference—you might like to serve more of a smaller selection of varieties. Prepare each vegetable separately as described, ready to reheat and serve. You will need a large pan of lightly salted water for blanching and a big bowl of ice water for refreshing. Make sure there's plenty of ice in the freezer to keep the refreshing water cool.* SERVES 2 AS A MAIN COURSE, 4 AS A LIGHT MEAL OR FIRST COURSE

Confit of tomatoes Heat the oven to its lowest setting. Dip the tomatoes into boiling water for 30 seconds or so, then into ice water. Drain and slip off the skins, then cut into quarters and remove the seeds. Lay cut-side down in a shallow roasting pan and cover with olive oil. Add slivers of garlic, and thyme and basil sprigs. Heat in the oven for about 1½ hours until the flesh is soft but still intact. Season and let cool in the oil, then drain well.

Asparagus Trim the base of the stalks and peel the lower third with a swivel vegetable peeler. Blanch the spears in boiling water for 2 minutes, then remove to a bowl of ice water.

Braised lettuce Halve lengthwise and sauté, cut-side down, in a little olive oil for 1 to 2 minutes. Season, then pour in vegetable nage to a depth of ½ inch (1 cm). Cover with buttered parchment paper and cook on a medium heat for 5 minutes until just tender (the nage will have reduced down to a glaze). Cool.

Peas and fava beans Shell these and slip the fava beans out of their skins. Blanch for 2 minutes and refresh in ice water.

Baby artichokes Trim the stalks and halve the artichoke hearts lengthwise. Drop into cold water acidulated with the ascorbic acid powder or lemon juice. Drain and pat dry when ready to cook. Heat a little olive oil in a small frying pan and sauté the artichokes for 2 to 3 minutes. Pour in 1¼ cups (300 ml) vegetable nage and simmer for 15 to 20 minutes until tender. Remove and cool slightly, then scrape out the small hairy choke in the middle. Cool and pat dry.

Baby turnips Blanch for 3 minutes or until just tender, then refresh.

Sautéed mushrooms Trim the stem bases, rinse the mushrooms quickly in cold water, drain, and pat dry. Heat a thin layer of olive oil in a pan and sauté the mushrooms over a high heat until just tender. Season lightly and set aside.

To serve Reheat the asparagus, turnips, lettuce, peas, and fava beans quickly in a little hot nage with a little butter for up to 1 minute. Sauté the artichokes and mushrooms separately and briefly in a little olive oil until hot. The tomatoes can be served at room temperature. Reheat the velouté. Arrange the vegetables on serving plates and accompany with the velouté.

2–3 plum tomatoes

2 fat garlic cloves, thinly sliced

2 thyme sprigs

2 basil sprigs

7 oz (200 g) green or white asparagus spears, or a mixture

2 romaine hearts

⅔ cup (100 g) shelled fresh peas or baby fava beans, or a mixture

4 baby artichoke hearts

6–8 baby turnips, quartered unless tiny

7 oz (200 g) mixed mushrooms (such as chanterelles, morels, shitake and oysters)

sea salt and freshly ground black pepper

For cooking:

olive oil

2½ cups (600 ml) Vegetable Nage (page 211), plus extra for reheating

a little butter

1 teaspoon ascorbic acid powder, or juice of 1 lemon

Thyme Velouté (page 212)

vegetables à la grecque

A SIMPLE SELECTION OF MY FAVORITE VEGETABLES, *blanched or lightly fried, then cooled in a balsamic dressing. It's very versatile—serve as a first course, as an accompaniment to steaks or chops, or as a vegetarian main dish.* SERVES 4 AS A FIRST COURSE OR ACCOMPANIMENT, 2 AS A MAIN COURSE

2 salsify, trimmed

juice of ½ lemon

2 globe artichokes

4 oz (100 g) snow peas, trimmed

3 tablespoons olive oil

2 carrots, thinly sliced

1 large or 3 small shallots, sliced

2 baby leeks, chopped

1 teaspoon coriander seeds, crushed

3 tablespoons Vinaigrette (page 218)

2 tablespoons balsamic vinegar

1 tablespoon chopped cilantro leaves

sea salt and freshly ground black pepper

Peel the salsify thinly, then cut into small batons (or thick julienne strips) and place in a bowl of cold water acidulated with the lemon juice.

Prepare the artichokes—only the hearts are used: To expose them, cut off the stalks and pull off all the leaves until you reach the hairy choke. Using a small, sharp knife, peel around the base of the heart. Then turn the heart on its side and, using a heavy cook's knife, cut straight down above the heart to remove the hairy fibers of the choke. Scrape off any stray choke with a teaspoon. Cut the artichoke hearts into batons and add to the acidulated water. Halve the snow peas crosswise.

Bring a large pan of salted water to a boil. Add the salsify and artichoke batons and boil for 2 to 3 minutes until just tender, but still retaining a good bite. Remove with a slotted spoon and plunge into a bowl of ice water to cool.

Add the snow peas to the boiling water and blanch for 1 minute, then drain and add to the ice water to refresh. Drain the cooled vegetables and shake dry.

Heat the olive oil in a large frying pan and sauté the carrots, shallot, and leeks with the crushed coriander for 2 to 3 minutes until just softened.

Stir in the blanched vegetables and heat for a minute or so. Add the vinaigrette and stir for a few seconds, then drizzle the balsamic vinegar over the vegetables. Check the seasoning and serve sprinkled with chopped cilantro.

SALSIFY *This ugly vegetable, also called oyster plant, doesn't look particularly inviting, but it has a good flavor. Peel away the dark outer skin to reveal a pale, creamy flesh that resembles white asparagus. As soon as you peel the salsify, immerse it in acidulated water (with lemon juice or ascorbic acid powder added), otherwise it will turn brown.*

fricassée of wild mushrooms

WILD MUSHROOMS HAVE DISTINCTIVE INDIVIDUAL FLAVORS *that shine through in this incredibly easy, elegant accompaniment. Make your selection according to the season and the best looking varieties on sale. Fresh wild mushrooms often contain grit and debris, so you need to wash and dry them carefully before cooking.* SERVES 4 AS AN ACCOMPANIMENT

First, pick over the wild mushrooms and trim the ends. Slice larger ones, if necessary. Soak for a few minutes in a bowl of tepid water, swishing with your hands so all forest debris sinks to the bottom. Drain and shake well, then pat dry in a large, clean dish towel or paper towels. If not using immediately, spread out the mushrooms on a tray and keep them, uncovered, in the refrigerator.

Heat the olive oil in a large frying pan, add the shallot, and sauté gently for 3 minutes until softened.

Add the butter and, when it has melted and starts to foam, toss in the cleaned mushrooms. Sauté for about 5 minutes until they are softened. Season to taste, then mix in the cream and cook for a minute or so.

Serve the mushroom fricassée as an accompaniment to grilled or broiled meats and fish.

10 oz (300 g) mixed wild mushrooms (such as chanterelles and morels), or shitake and oyster mushrooms
2 tablespoons olive oil
1 shallot, minced
2 tablespoons (25 g) butter
½ cup (100 ml) heavy cream
sea salt and freshly ground black pepper

CHEF'S TIP *Wild mushrooms can be expensive, but you can make a delicious fricassée with a combination of fresh wild mushrooms and cultivated crimini mushrooms. Alternatively, you could use half cultivated mushrooms with just one wild variety, adding some soaked dried porcini to beef up the flavor.*

asian pear waldorf salad

CREATED IN THE WALDORF ASTORIA *in the 1890s by Oscar Tshirky, the Maitre D' at the time, this has been a classic American salad ever since. I have enhanced the original recipe with the addition of Asian pears, a fruit I admire for its crisp clean taste and fantastic texture.* SERVES 4 AS A STARTER

½ cup (125 ml) water

2 tablespoons lemon juice

2 firm, ripe pears (such as Bosc or
   Anjou)

2 Asian pears

2 celery stalks, finely sliced

2 carrots, halved and finely sliced

1 cup (100 g) walnut halves

1 cup (150 g) golden raisins

1 cup (250 ml) Mayonnaise (page
   219)

5 tablespoons lime juice

1 tablespoon Dijon mustard

¼ cup mint leaves

sea salt and freshly ground black
   pepper

Put the water and lemon juice into a large mixing bowl. Halve and core all of the pears, and cut into ½-inch (1-cm) pieces. Immediately place in the acidulated water and leave for 10 minutes.

Drain the pears and place in a clean bowl with the celery, carrots, walnuts, and raisins. Add the mayonnaise, lime juice, mustard, and salt and pepper to taste. Toss gently to mix, then cover and place in the refrigerator for 1 hour.

Add the mint leaves, and toss the salad again before serving.

CHEF'S TIP *The secret here is to immerse the fruit in acidulated water as soon as you prepare it, to prevent discoloration. We use this technique a lot for vegetables such as Jerusalem artichokes and salsify as well as fruit. Vitamin C powder (ascorbic acid) can be used instead of lemon juice.*

roasted baby beet salad

SWEET, TENDER, BABY BEETS *have a wonderful earthy taste. Cook them my way to bring out their full flavor—bake whole (unpeeled) on a bed of rock salt in a foil parcel, then peel, sauté in butter to glaze, and dress in good aged balsamic vinegar. I serve the baby beets warm or at room temperature with lamb or with oily fish, such as salmon or mackerel. (Illustrated on pages 122 and 123)* SERVES 4 AS AN ACCOMPANIMENT

Preheat the oven to 350°F (180°C). Wash the baby beets and trim the tops, leaving on a little of the leafy stems and roots. Pat dry.

Lay a large sheet of foil on a baking sheet and spread the rock salt in the center. Nestle the beets in the rock salt and scatter with thyme, tearing the stems into smaller sprigs. Scrunch the foil and bring the edges together to enclose the beets and seal.

Bake for about 15 to 20 minutes until the baby beets are tender. Remove, uncover, and let cool slightly. Wearing a pair of thin rubber gloves (to avoid staining your hands), peel the beets while they are still warm, using a thin-bladed knife. Cut each beet in half vertically.

Heat the butter in a sauté pan. When it starts to foam, toss in the beets and cook, turning frequently, for a couple of minutes until coated in butter and glossy. Add the balsamic vinegar to deglaze, and bubble until reduced and syrupy. Serve warm or at room temperature.

1 lb (500 g) baby beets
about 1½ cups (200 g) rock salt
2–3 thyme sprigs
3½ tablespoons (50 g) butter
3–4 tablespoons balsamic vinegar

CHEF'S TIP *If baby beets are not available, buy the smallest fresh beets you can find and increase the baking time accordingly. After peeling, cut the beets into slices about ½ inch (1 cm) thick before glazing.*

CHEF'S SECRET *Baking beets in their skins on a bed of salt is a great way to draw out some of the moisture, to concentrate and intensify the flavor of the vegetable. The skin protects the beet flesh and prevents it from becoming salty. As you peel away the skin after baking, you'll simply remove any traces of rock salt, leaving sweet, juicy beets.*

three bean salad with cumin

I LOVE THIS COMBINATION *of green, yellow wax and red kidney beans in a citrusy dressing. I suggest that you make this salad at least a day in advance, to give the flavors time to marry together—it just gets better and better.* SERVES 4 AS AN ACCOMPANIMENT

¼ cup (60 ml) lime juice

2 tablespoons sugar

½ cup (125 ml) olive oil

2 garlic cloves, minced

1 teaspoon ground cumin

8 oz (250 g) green beans cut into
  1-inch (2.5-cm) lengths

8 oz (250 g) yellow wax beans, cut
  into 1-inch (2.5-cm) lengths

15½ oz (440 g) can red kidney beans,
  drained

1 bunch scallions, trimmed and finely
  chopped

¼ cup (25 g) cilantro, finely chopped

2 medium oranges

sea salt and freshly ground black
  pepper

Put the lime juice, sugar, olive oil, garlic, cumin, and seasoning in a small non-reactive pan. Warm gently, stirring occasionally, until the sugar dissolves. Transfer this dressing to a large glass bowl and set aside to cool.

Bring 3 quarts (3 liters) water to a boil and season with salt. Have ready a bowl of ice water. Add the green and yellow beans to the boiling water and blanch for 3 to 4 minutes until just crisp. Drain and plunge the beans into the ice water to cool quickly. When cooled, drain well.

Add the blanched beans and kidney beans to the dressing with the scallions and chopped cilantro. Cover and leave to marinate in the refrigerator overnight.

Remove the salad from the refrigerator 30 minutes before serving. Peel the oranges, removing all white pith, then cut the segments free from the membrane. Stir the orange segments into the salad. Check the seasoning and toss the salad again before serving.

CHEF'S TIP *The secret of this salad is the intensity and freshness of the flavors. Buy fresh cilantro by the bunch if possible and chop the leaves just before adding them to the salad. The cumin also needs to be fresh and fragrant. It is important that you always keep your spices fresh. Store them in an airtight jar in a dark cupboard and be aware that spices do not have a long shelf life. I recommend that you replace them every year.*

cauliflower purée

CAULIFLOWER IS A VERSATILE VEGETABLE, *but it does emit a rather unpleasant aroma when you cook it in the usual way. To counter this, I simmer the florets in milk with herbs. You can strain off the milk and use it to make a béchamel sauce (see below), serving the florets as a simple accompaniment, or take the dish a stage farther, as I have here, cooking the cauliflower until really tender, then blending to a velvety-smooth purée. This purée makes a wonderful base for curry-dusted pan-fried fish or scallops.*
SERVES 6 AS AN ACCOMPANIMENT

Trim the cauliflower, discarding the leaves, and cut into florets. Place in a saucepan and add the milk, herbs, and about ½ teaspoon salt. Bring to a boil, then cover and simmer gently. (To serve the florets whole, as a simple accompaniment, drain after 5 to 7 minutes.) For a purée, cook for 12 to 15 minutes until very tender.

Drain the cauliflower, reserving the milk. Discard the herbs. Tip the florets into a blender or food processor. Whiz until very smooth, adding enough of the reserved milk to give a very creamy consistency, scraping down the sides a couple of times. You may need to blend the mixture for up to 5 minutes to achieve a really smooth, silky texture.

Taste and adjust the seasoning, adding a little pepper, if required. Serve piping hot.

1 head cauliflower
1¼ cups (300 ml) milk
1 small bay leaf
1 thyme sprig
sea salt and freshly ground white pepper

COOK'S TIP *The milk in which the cauliflower is cooked can be used for a béchamel sauce: Make the butter-and-flour roux in the usual way, then incorporate the flavored milk and cook, stirring, until smooth.*

fondue of lettuce

IF YOU HAVE NEVER EATEN COOKED LETTUCE, *I urge you to try it! Cooked in light, buttery stock, this salad vegetable is surprisingly delicious and makes an excellent accompaniment to poultry and fish. And because it is tender and creamy, you won't need to make a special sauce or gravy to go with the meal. Small romaine hearts, with their tightly packed leaves, are the best choice here—allow one per person.*
SERVES 4 AS AN ACCOMPANIMENT

4 romaine hearts

2 tablespoons olive oil

5 tablespoons (75 g) butter, cut in cubes

7 fl oz (200 ml) Chicken Stock
  (page 210)

1 thyme sprig

sea salt and freshly ground black pepper

Cut the romaine hearts in half lengthwise. Don't cut out the cores. Carefully wash, then pat dry with paper towels.

Heat the olive oil in a sauté pan. When it is really hot, lay the lettuce halves in the pan, cut-side down. Season and cook over a medium heat for about 2 minutes until lightly caramelized.

Gradually add the butter in pieces and the stock, then scatter in the thyme, torn into tiny sprigs. Cover the lettuce with a buttered sheet of parchment paper. Cook on a low heat for about 8 minutes, basting once or twice, until the lettuce is tender but still holds its shape. The liquid should have reduced to a glossy glaze by now. Let stand for 5 minutes before serving.

CHEF'S TIP *Frying the lettuce halves first in hot olive oil caramelizes the outer leaves and gives them a succulent, sweet flavor. Braising them in light stock with butter thereafter enhances the flavor and lends a creamy texture.*

braised red cabbage with juniper

THE SIMPLEST COOKING TECHNIQUES ARE OFTEN THE BEST. *Here, red cabbage is cooked long and slow, yet obligingly retains its texture and color. It can even be made ahead and reheated without loss of flavor. Don't be tempted to use the more refined wine vinegar—for this dish, malt vinegar lends the appropriate flavor. However, the amount of sugar and butter can be adjusted to taste. I prefer it sweet and buttery. This dish is wonderful with roast pork, duck, and goose, and the holiday turkey.*
SERVES 6–8 AS AN ACCOMPANIMENT

1 head red cabbage, about 1 lb
  (500 g)
1 cup (250 ml) malt vinegar
½ cup (100 g) Demerara or other raw
  brown sugar
½ cup (125 g) butter, diced
1 teaspoon sea salt
2 star anise
½ teaspoon coriander seeds
10 juniper berries
freshly ground black pepper

Preheat the oven to 275°F (140°C). Quarter the cabbage and cut out the core. Pull off any outer leaves that are damaged or wilted, then shred each cabbage quarter as finely as possible, using a sharp knife or mandoline.

Place the cabbage in a large, cast-iron casserole. Add the vinegar, sugar, butter, and salt. Tie the star anise, coriander seeds, and juniper berries in a small square of cheesecloth and nestle in the center of the cabbage.

Cover the casserole. A good seal is essential, so if the lid isn't tight-fitting, cover the casserole with foil, then put the lid on. Cook in the oven for up to 3 hours, until the cabbage is tender, giving it a good stir halfway through cooking.

When the cabbage is tender, check to see if any juices remain. If so, strain them into a pan and boil down to reduce until syrupy, then stir back into the casserole. Discard the bag of spices and adjust the seasoning before serving.

JUNIPER BERRIES *These dark blue berries have a sweet, aromatic flavor, reminiscent of pine. They have a natural affinity with cabbage, and are often used to flavor rich meat and game dishes.*

corn fritters with lime crème fraîche

THIS IS THE PERFECT CORN FRITTER. *Crisp and golden on the outside, yet deliciously creamy and soft in the center, it is bursting with the nutty flavor of fresh corn. Topped with a tangy lime crème fraîche, it makes a delicious snack or appetizer.*
SERVES 4 AS A STARTER OR SNACK

Place the corn kernels in a medium bowl, and add the egg, flour, cornmeal, and milk. Mix well and then season with the cayenne, cumin, and salt and pepper to taste. Let the batter rest for at least 1 hour, or up to 4 hours if preparing ahead.

For the lime crème fraîche, mix the crème fraîche with the lime juice and season with salt and pepper to taste. Set aside until ready to serve.

To cook the fritters, heat the oil in a large heavy-bottomed skillet over a medium heat. When the oil begins to shimmer, drop tablespoonfuls of the batter into the pan, spacing them well apart. Fry for about 1 minute until golden brown on the underside, then turn the fritters over and cook for a further 30 to 50 seconds. Transfer the fritters to a plate lined with paper towel and continue until you have used all of the batter.

Place 3 or 4 corn fritters on each plate and top with a spoonful of crème fraîche. Dust with a little paprika or cayenne, scatter with a few chives and serve immediately.

½ cup (85 g) fresh corn kernels
1 large egg, beaten
3 tablespoons all-purpose flour
3 tablespoons cornmeal
3 tablespoons milk
¼ teaspoon cayenne pepper
¼ teaspoon ground cumin
½ cup crème fraîche
juice of 1 lime
¼ cup vegetable or corn oil
sea salt and freshly ground black pepper
paprika or extra cayenne pepper, for dusting
chives, for serving

sautéed broccoli with crispy garlic

BROCCOLI IS A HIGHLY VERSATILE VEGETABLE *and very popular, but it is so easily overcooked. One minute it is too hard, the next it is unpalatably limp and watery. My solution is to blanch the florets briefly in boiling water, then immediately refresh them in ice water. When ready to serve, I stir-fry the broccoli quickly—here, it is served Chinese-style with a contrast of crisp garlic slivers. It's an ideal accompaniment for fish or chicken.* SERVES 4 AS AN ACCOMPANIMENT

1 large head broccoli, about 1 lb (500 g)

2 tablespoons sunflower or olive oil

2 fat garlic cloves, thinly sliced

1 tablespoon roasted sesame oil

1 onion, thinly sliced

2 tablespoons oyster sauce

sea salt and freshly ground black pepper

Cut off the main stem, then cut the broccoli into small florets. Have ready a large bowl of ice water.

Bring a large pan of salted water to a boil, add the broccoli florets, and blanch for 2 minutes, timing from the moment the water returns to a boil. Immediately drain the broccoli and tip into the bowl of ice water to refresh. Drain and set aside until ready to serve.

Heat 1 tablespoon sunflower or olive oil in a frying pan. When it is hot, add the garlic slivers and sauté until golden brown and crisp. Do not allow to scorch or the garlic will taste bitter. Immediately remove with a slotted spoon and drain on paper towels.

When ready to serve, heat the remaining sunflower or olive oil in the pan, together with the sesame oil. Add the onion slices and sauté over a medium heat for about 5 minutes until softened.

Add the broccoli florets and sauté until piping hot, tossing carefully to ensure the florets are not broken up. Mix in the oyster sauce, then add the crisp garlic slivers. Adjust the seasoning and serve immediately.

REFRESHING *This is an important technique that helps to preserve the vibrant color and freshness of vegetables, by preventing them from overcooking. It's especially useful for fast-cooking green vegetables like broccoli. All you need is plenty of ice water—add three big handfuls of ice cubes to a large bowl of cold water. As soon as you drain the vegetables from the boiling water, immediately plunge them into the ice water. Leave for about 5 minutes to cool thoroughly, then drain the vegetables and set aside, ready to reheat and serve. The water can be used again. Simply replenish the ice cubes.*

CHEF'S TIP *Blanching baby onions in boiling water for 30 seconds to 1 minute will loosen their skins and make it much easier to peel them. However, for this dish, you will find that the onions won't caramelize as successfully if they have been pre-blanched, so avoid doing so unless you are very short of time.*

caramelized baby onions with beet jus

HERE, BABY ONIONS, OR SHALLOTS, *are cooked in a beet "jus" until they take on a rich magenta glaze, then served as an accompaniment in their own right, rather than used merely as a flavoring ingredient. Make your own jus if you have a juicer, using raw beets, or buy bottled beet juice from a wholefood market.* SERVES 4–6 AS AN ACCOMPANIMENT

If using fresh beets, peel them, wearing thin rubber gloves to prevent your fingers from being stained. Chop roughly and whiz through your juicer. If using bottled beet juice, strain through a fine sieve so the liquid is clear. You need about 7 fl oz (200 ml) juice.

Heat the butter in a large sauté pan. When it starts to foam, add the whole baby onions or shallots, along with the thyme and sugar, and cook for about 5 minutes until lightly caramelized. Season with salt and pepper as they cook.

Pour in the beet juice and stock or vegetable nage. Bring to a boil, then cook uncovered for a further 5 minutes, stirring occasionally, until the onions are just tender; they should still retain a bite. Using a slotted spoon, transfer the onions to a dish.

Bubble up the pan juices until reduced to a syrupy glaze. Return the onions to the pan and heat through, turning to coat with the glaze. Discard the thyme before serving.

1 large, fresh beet (about 8 oz/250 g) or 7 fl oz (200 ml) bottled beet juice

7 tablespoons (100 g) butter

8 oz (250 g) baby onions or small shallots, peeled

few thyme sprigs

½ teaspoon sugar

½ cup (100 ml) Chicken Stock (page 210) or Vegetable Nage (page 211)

sea salt and freshly ground black pepper

parsnip chips

BEYOND POTATOES, *I think parsnips make the best deep-fried chips. To create wafer-thin, broad ribbons, buy older parsnips rather than young ones. You'll also need a swivel vegetable peeler. A light dusting of curry salt makes them irresistible, but you may prefer to omit this if serving the chips as an accompaniment rather than a snack. They go particularly well with venison, beef steaks, and game birds.* SERVES 4 AS AN ACCOMPANIMENT

4 parsnips

vegetable oil for deep-frying,
    about 2 cups (500 ml)

about 1 teaspoon curry salt
    (see right)

Peel the parsnips, then trim the ends. Using a swivel vegetable peeler, mandoline, or Japanese vegetable slicer, shave each parsnip lengthwise into wafer-thin slices.

Pour the oil into a deep-fat fryer or deep, heavy saucepan; it should one-third fill the pan. Heat the oil until it registers 350°F (180°C) on a frying thermometer, or until a small cube of day-old bread dropped into the oil browns in 30 seconds.

Deep-fry the parsnip slices, a handful at a time: Using a slotted spoon, add them to the oil and deep-fry for 2 to 3 minutes until golden brown and crisp. As they fry, keep moving the parsnip chips around in the pan with the back of the spoon to ensure an even color.

Remove and drain on paper towels, then immediately sprinkle the chips with the curry salt while they are still piping hot, so the flavor is readily absorbed. Keep warm in a low oven, uncovered, while you cook the remaining chips. Return the oil to the correct temperature in between frying each batch.

Serve the parsnip chips as soon as you have cooked them all.

CURRY SALT *This has so many uses, it's worth making more than you need and storing the rest in a small jar. I sprinkle it onto scallops, shrimp, fish, and chicken, to enhance their flavor. To prepare, simply mix 1 teaspoon medium curry powder with 2 teaspoons fine sea salt.*

pomme purée

THERE ARE THREE SECRETS *to a velvety-smooth pomme purée. The first is the choice of potato. You need a baking or all-purpose potato with a good flavor and floury or mealy texture. Then, to make sure the potato cooks evenly, cut it into chunks of the same size. Finally, press the potato through a food mill or potato ricer, rather than mash or beat it, to achieve a silky, even texture. To keep it light, add hot cream and beat in diced butter. Serve plain, or try one of my suggested flavorings below.*
SERVES 4–6 AS AN ACCOMPANIMENT

2¼ lb (1 kg) baking or all-purpose
   potatoes
⅔ cup (150 ml) heavy cream
4–6 tablespoons (60–90 g) butter, cut
   into small cubes
sea salt and freshly ground black pepper

Peel the potatoes thinly, then cut in even-sized, 2-inch (5-cm) chunks. Add to a pan of lightly salted water and bring to a boil. Simmer until tender, allowing about 15 minutes from the moment the water returns to a boil, but check after 12 minutes.

Drain the potatoes, then return to the pan over the heat to dry out for a few minutes. Pass the potatoes through a food mill or press through a potato ricer.

Boil the cream in a small pan until reduced by half. Stir into the potatoes and season with salt and pepper to taste. Gradually work in the cubes of butter, according to how rich you want the purée to be. A good pomme purée will be able to take a lot of butter without "splitting." Keep warm, or chill until required and then reheat in a pan or microwave to serve.

FLAVORINGS

Horseradish Add 2 to 3 tablespoons horseradish relish to the finished purée.
Mustard Add 1 tablespoon coarse grain mustard and 1 teaspoon horseradish relish to the finished purée.
Truffle Add a few drops of truffle oil to the finished purée. Serve sprinkled with a little minced black truffle, if available.
Celeriac Peel and chop ½ small head celeriac, about 8 oz (250 g), and cook in lightly salted boiling water until tender. Drain and whiz in a blender or food processor until velvety smooth. Mix into the pomme purée with the cream and seasoning.
Basil Heat 4 large basil leaves in the cream as you boil to reduce it. Remove the basil before mixing the cream into the pomme purée.

pommes dauphinoise

FOR THIS CREAMY POTATO GRATIN, *you need to buy a waxy, boiling variety that will retain its texture as it absorbs liquid. A traditional gratin is cooked entirely in the oven, but I prefer to simmer the potatoes first in milk on the stovetop, then finish the dish in the oven. This method cuts the cooking time and gives you a more dependable result. The potatoes should be of a similar size.* SERVES 4 AS AN ACCOMPANIMENT

Preheat the oven to 400°F (200°C). Peel the potatoes thinly, then cut into even, ½-inch (1-cm) slices. Bring the milk and cream to a boil in a large saucepan and add the garlic, herbs, and seasoning. Simmer for a couple of minutes.

Slide the potatoes into the pan and stir gently. Simmer for about 7 minutes until the potato slices are only just tender; they should hold their shape and retain a bite. Drain the par-cooked potatoes in a colander set over a bowl to catch the creamy milk.

Layer the potatoes in a shallow baking dish, sprinkling two-thirds of the cheese and seasoning in between the layers. Trickle a little of the saved milk over each layer too.

Pour a little more of the milk around the sides, but not too much—just enough to moisten. Sprinkle the last of the cheese over the top.

Place the dish in a shallow roasting pan and bake for about 10 to 15 minutes or until the cheese is beginning to bubble and turn golden brown. Let stand for 10 minutes before serving.

1¼ lb (600 g) slightly waxy boiling
  potatoes
1½ cups (350 ml) milk
1½ cups (350 ml) heavy cream
1 large garlic clove, sliced
1 thyme sprig
1 bay leaf
scant ½ cup (90 g) shredded Gruyère
  cheese
sea salt and freshly ground black pepper

CHEF'S TIP *Making sure the potatoes are just cooked before you layer them takes the guesswork out of this classic baked potato dish and ensures that it is always creamy with a nice texture.*

EGGS

WHERE WOULD WE BE WITHOUT EGGS? *The versatility of this indispensable ingredient never ceases to amaze me—a food scientist's dream. Not only do eggs thicken and enrich sauces, bind stuffings, and lighten and expand on whisking to create soufflés and meringues, they can also be cooked in a variety of ways to serve as a meal in their own right. I have fond memories of the egg "sarnies" my mother packed into my lunchbox for school outings. No one sat next to me because of the smell, but I didn't care—they tasted great.*

Our eggs are always free-range because the flavor is better. A couple of fresh eggs, a bit of butter, and a handful of chopped herbs, and you always have a meal. Or, in the case of Le Gavroche, it's a couple of the finest fresh eggs scrambled slowly with butter, piled onto toasted Poilane bread, topped with sliced fresh porcini, and served with a fresh tomato purée and torn basil leaves.

Recently I have discovered the delights of duck eggs. Not only are the yolks naturally brighter yellow and larger than hens' eggs, but the whites also have a superior flavor. Duck eggs are fabulous with fresh asparagus and they make the best cakes. Goose eggs are also great in cakes, though like rare gulls' eggs, they are seasonal. Quail eggs are farmed and sold year round.

One word of warning, if you think you might have a reaction to lightly cooked eggs, then avoid recipes that use raw or lightly set eggs. We use the freshest eggs possible from quality farmers and recommend you do the same.

eggs benedict with minted hollandaise

In 1894, a Wall Street broker, *Lemuel Benedict, ordered the chef at New York's Waldorf Hotel to put together all his favorite foods—eggs, bacon, toast, and hollandaise—to cure a hangover. A century on, with muffins instead of toast and a minted hollandaise, this is still one of our popular breakfast dishes at Claridges. We poach the eggs ahead and keep the hollandaise warm in a bain marie, because it cannot be reheated once it has cooled and solidified.* SERVES 4 AS A LIGHT MEAL

4 extra large eggs

2 English muffins, split

1 tablespoon (15 g) butter

4–8 slices prosciutto

Minted hollandaise:

⅔ cup (150 g) unsalted butter

2 large egg yolks

6 coriander seeds, crushed

1½ teaspoons reduced white wine
    vinegar (see below)

squeeze of lemon juice

pinch of cayenne pepper

4 large mint leaves, cut into thin
    julienne strips

sea salt

REDUCED WINE VINEGAR *It's useful to keep a small bottle of this in the refrigerator. To prepare, pour 1 cup (250 ml) white wine vinegar into a saucepan and add ½ small shallot, sliced, a blade of mace, and ¼ teaspoon black peppercorns. Boil until reduced by half, then strain, let cool, and pour into a small bottle.*

To make the hollandaise, melt the butter in a pan over a gentle heat, then carefully pour off the clear, golden butter into a pitcher; discard the milky solids. Set the clarified butter aside to cool until lukewarm.

Put the egg yolks, crushed coriander, and 1 tablespoon cold water into a heatproof bowl and fit snugly over a pan of gently simmering water. Using an immersion blender or electric beater, beat until very light and frothy (this makes it easier to incorporate the butter).

Remove the bowl from the heat and continue beating for 2 to 3 minutes, then slowly trickle in the clarified butter as you continue to beat. Don't add the butter too quickly or the sauce will curdle. When all the butter is incorporated, season with salt and add the reduced vinegar, lemon juice, and cayenne. Finally, fold in the chopped mint. Set the bowl back over the pan of hot water (but off the heat) to keep warm; stir occasionally to prevent a skin from forming. If the sauce does happen to split, whisk in a trickle of cold water to re-emulsify it.

Poach the eggs (see below). You can do this in advance for convenience, and to avoid overcooking them.

To assemble, toast the split muffins lightly on both sides. If you have poached the eggs ahead, using a slotted spoon, transfer them to a pan containing enough boiling hot buttery water to cover. Let stand off the heat for 15 to 20 seconds (no longer or the yolks won't be soft). Remove with a slotted spoon and drain well.

Butter the muffins and place on warmed plates. Arrange 1 or 2 slices of prosciutto on each muffin, sit a poached egg on top, and coat with the warm hollandaise. Serve immediately.

POACHING EGGS TO PERFECTION *It is absolutely essential to use very fresh eggs to ensure the whites hold together. Half-fill a shallow saucepan with water, add a dash of vinegar, and bring to a steady simmer. Meanwhile, break an egg into a cup. To help the egg set to a neat shape, lightly whisk the water, using a slow circular movement, then reduce the heat to a low simmer. Slide the egg into the pan and poach for 1½ minutes. Carefully lift out and place in a bowl of chilled water to stop the cooking. Repeat with the remaining eggs. Keep refrigerated until needed.*

fried duck eggs with asparagus

A DUCK EGG IS ABOUT 25 PERCENT LARGER THAN A HEN'S EGG, *with a bright yellow, rich, creamy yolk that stands proud of the white. Duck eggs are superb fried, but the frying must be gentle, almost as a confit technique, so the egg white sets without becoming crisp. Ideally, you need two blini pans, each about 5 inches (12 cm) in diameter. Alternatively, you can use the smallest frying pan you have in the kitchen. This is a great dish to cook when homegrown asparagus starts to appear in the market, in early spring.* SERVES 2 AS A LIGHT MEAL

7 oz (200 g) green asparagus spears

good olive oil, for drizzling and frying

3 tablespoons (40 g) butter, cut into
   thin flakes

2 duck eggs, or 2 jumbo hen's eggs

about 1 oz (30 g) Parmesan cheese,
   finely pared into shavings

handful of arugula leaves, about
   1 oz (25 g)

sea salt and freshly coarse ground
   black pepper

Peel the lower stalks of the asparagus, using a swivel peeler. Bring a pan of lightly salted water to a boil and blanch the spears for 1 minute. Drain and refresh in a bowl of ice water for 5 minutes, then drain and pat dry. Place the blanched asparagus in a shallow dish, drizzle with olive oil, and turn to coat.

Pour 1 tablespoon olive oil into each of two 5-inch (12-cm) blini pans, add a little butter, and place over a medium heat. When you can feel a gentle heat rising, crack a duck egg into each pan and fry gently until cooked to perfection (see below). Duck eggs will take 8 to 10 minutes, hen's eggs 5 to 6 minutes.

In the meantime, heat a grill pan over a high heat until you can feel a good heat rising, then add the asparagus spears and cook for about 2 to 3 minutes, turning occasionally, until tender and lightly charred.

To serve, arrange the asparagus on two warmed, large plates and season. Scatter on the Parmesan shavings and arugula leaves, dressing these very lightly with olive oil, if desired. Carefully place a fried egg on top, coarsely grind on some pepper, and serve straight away.

PERFECT FRIED EGGS
Crack the egg into the hot oiled pan over a medium heat. Tilt the pan to center the yolk—it will set in position after about 30 seconds. Lower the heat and cook until the white starts to firm, about 4 minutes for duck eggs, 3 minutes for jumbo hen's eggs. Slip the butter flakes down the side of the pan. As the butter begins to foam, spoon it over the egg whites to help them cook. Season lightly and cook until the whites are just set firm and the yolks are still a bit soft. Loosen the edge with a small metal spatula and remove.

smoked salmon and scrambled egg tartlets

SCRAMBLED EGGS ARE A MATTER OF PERSONAL TASTE. *I like them creamy and fine-textured, achieved by preparing them in the classic way. For an elegant light meal, I line crisp pastry tartlets with smoked salmon, fill them with warm scrambled eggs, and top with a little caviar—Osietra is my preferred choice. For a less extravagant finish, you can simply top with smoked salmon strips and snipped chives. To treat the palate to an unforgettable experience, serve the caviar-topped tartlets with a swirl of reduced lobster bisque.* SERVES 4 AS A FIRST COURSE OR LIGHT MEAL

First, make the tartlet shells: Cut the pastry into four, then roll out each portion thinly to a round and use to line four 4-inch (10-cm) tartlet molds with removable bases. Bring the pastry high up the sides, so it extends about ½ inch (1 cm) above the rim. Prick the pastry with a fork. Carefully stack the pastry-lined molds, one on top of the other—this helps keeps the pastry thin and crisp as it bakes. Line the exposed top tartlet shell with foil and ceramic beans. Let the stack of tart shells rest in the refrigerator for 15 minutes.

Preheat the oven to 400°F (200°C). Place the tartlet molds, still in a stack, on a heavy baking sheet and bake for about 15 minutes until golden brown. Remove the foil and ceramic beans, and carefully separate the tartlet molds. Trim the pastry edges level with the rim of the molds, using a sharp knife. Return to the oven to bake for 3 to 5 minutes to crisp the pastry.

In the meantime, if serving lobster bisque, boil to reduce by half; keep warm.

When ready to serve, make the scrambled eggs: Put the butter into a wide, shallow pan over a low heat. As it begins to melt, add the eggs and whisk vigorously with a balloon whisk as they start to heat. When the eggs begin to scramble, pour in the cream and milk. Immediately remove from the heat, season, and stir gently with a fork until creamy.

Remove the tartlet shells from the molds. Line the sides with the smoked salmon, so it extends high above the rims. Place on warmed serving plates and fill with the warm scrambled eggs. Top with a spoonful of caviar and surround each tartlet with a drizzle of reduced lobster bisque, if desired. Alternatively, simply top with a few smoked salmon strips and snipped chives. Serve at once.

12 oz (350 g) puff pastry, homemade (page 184) or bought
3 tablespoons (40 g) butter, diced
6 extra large or 8 large eggs
4 tablespoons heavy cream
4 tablespoons milk
5 oz (150 g) sliced smoked salmon
sea salt and freshly ground black pepper

For serving:
7 fl oz (200 ml) Lobster Bisque (page 12, optional)
4 teaspoons caviar, or extra strips of smoked salmon and snipped chives

CLASSIC SCRAMBLED EGGS *Use a wide, shallow pan set over a medium heat to begin with. Add the butter and, as soon as it starts to melt, crack in the eggs. Using a balloon whisk, beat vigorously until the eggs form soft curds, then whisk in the cream and milk. This will slow the "cuisson" down and achieve the correct creamy texture. Season at this stage, not before, and continue to stir gently until the eggs are soft and creamy. Serve without delay.*

cobb salad with quail eggs

COBB SALAD ORIGINATED IN HOLLYWOOD *in the 1920s. It was created at the Brown Derby restaurant and named after Bob Cobb, the manager. My version is somewhat different and uses quail eggs rather than hen's eggs. Note that the presentation of this dish is paramount to its success.* SERVES 4 AS A LIGHT MEAL

½ cup (125 ml) dry white wine

juice of 1 lemon

5 thyme sprigs

2 skinless chicken breasts

6 quail eggs

8 oz (250 g) Canadian bacon slices

3 tablespoons Vinaigrette (page 218)

2 avocados

1 large romaine lettuce

12 cherry tomatoes, halved

8 oz (250 g) blue cheese, crumbled
   into pieces

1 scallion, trimmed and sliced

sea salt and freshly ground black
   pepper

Put the wine into a large pan with the juice of ½ lemon, the thyme, and seasoning. Add the chicken breasts, then pour in just enough water to cover them. Bring to a boil and remove any scum from the surface with a slotted spoon. Reduce the heat to a simmer and cook for 10 minutes.

Remove the pan from the heat and let the chicken cool in the poaching liquid (it will finish cooking in the residual heat).

Meanwhile, cook the quail eggs in a small pan of boiling water for 2½ minutes. Drain and cool under running water, then peel away the shells, and cut the quail eggs in half. Broil the bacon slices for a few minutes on each side until crisp, then drain on paper towel, and break into large pieces.

Take the chicken out of the liquid and cut into bite-sized pieces. Place in a bowl, add 2 tablespoons of the vinaigrette, and toss to mix. Halve the avocados, peel, and pit, then chop the flesh and toss in the remaining lemon juice to prevent discoloration.

Tear the lettuce leaves into small pieces and divide among four serving plates. Pile the chicken in the center of each plate. Arrange the cherry tomatoes, quail eggs, avocado, blue cheese, bacon, and scallion on top. Drizzle with the remaining vinaigrette and serve at once.

CHEF'S SECRET *I keep a supply of my own vinaigrette in a squeezy bottle in the fridge at all times. I use a combination of olive oil and a milder flavored oil, such as sunflower or peanut, to ensure a light vinaigrette that does not overpower the taste of the dish. This is especially important when you are dressing delicately flavored food, such as quail eggs, shellfish, or fish.*

perfect cheese omelet

IN THEORY, IT'S EASY TO MAKE AN OMELET, *but the timing is critical. The perfect omelet is pale golden on the outside without the slightest tinge of brown, and soft and creamy in the center, which the French term "bauvese." If overcooked, an omelet will be hard and leathery, and quite unpalatable. The secret lies in the technique of constantly stirring and shaking the pan during cooking, then folding and tipping the omelet straight onto a warmed serving plate so it folds neatly into three.*
SERVES 1 AS A LIGHT MEAL

Place an 8- to 8½-inch (20- to 21-cm) omelet pan over a medium-high heat. Beat the eggs in a bowl until evenly blended, but don't add salt or pepper at this stage. Add the olive oil to the pan and, when you can feel a good heat rising, slip in the butter and swirl it in the pan as it foams and melts.

Pour in the beaten eggs and swirl them around in the pan with a fork, shaking the pan frequently with one hand. The trick is to get the eggs to an even, light, creamy texture at this stage.

When the mixture is three-fourths set, stop stirring with the fork and leave undisturbed for 30 seconds or so, until the base of the omelet is just set. Loosen the edges with a metal spatula.

Wrap your free hand in a clean dish towel, hold the pan just off the heat, tilt away from you, and bang the side opposite the handle on the surface a few times. This has the effect of shaking the omelet loose from the pan so that it begins to slide onto the edge farthest away from you.

At this point, season with salt and pepper and scatter on the cheese. Then, holding the pan handle again, flip the third of the omelet farthest from you into the center. Now hold the pan over a warmed plate and slide the omelet out, so it folds over into a neat roll. For real perfection, use your towel to shape the omelet roll neatly. And that's it. The heat of the creamy center is sufficient to melt the cheese. Serve at once.

3 large eggs
1 tablespoon olive oil
1 tablespoon (15 g) butter
¼ cup (50 g) shredded Gruyère or
    aged Cheddar cheese
sea salt and freshly ground black pepper

CHEF'S SECRET *Don't season the eggs before you cook them, because salt breaks down the albumen in the egg white and thins the mixture, giving a less satisfactory result.*

THE RIGHT TOOLS *The choice of pan is important. You need a frying pan about 8½ inches (21 cm) in diameter, with rounded sides that make it easier to flip the omelet. We use a heavy, nonstick pan that can take metal forks; if yours is not as robust, use a wooden or heatproof plastic fork for stirring.*

goat cheese and spinach omelet

AS A MODIFICATION OF THE PERFECT OMELET TECHNIQUE, *chunks of chèvre and baby spinach leaves are scattered on top of a soft-set omelet, which is then flashed under the broiler to lightly color the chèvre. I use a cendré (ash-coated) goat cheese, but you could substitute an herb-coated chèvre, if you prefer. Serve straight from the pan, with a mixed leaf salad and some crusty bread.* SERVES 2 AS A LIGHT MEAL

2 large handfuls of baby spinach
   leaves, about 2 oz (50 g)

2 tablespoons olive oil

4 extra large eggs

4 teaspoons (20 g) butter, diced

4 oz (100 g) good, soft chèvre
   (preferably cendré), with rind

2 tablespoons freshly grated Parmesan
   cheese

sea salt and freshly ground black pepper

Preheat the broiler. Put the spinach into a saucepan with 1 tablespoon olive oil and place over a low heat for about 30 seconds until lightly wilted, then remove from the heat and drain on paper towels. Tease the lightly cooked leaves apart to separate.

Place an 8- to 9-inch (21- to 23-cm) omelet pan over a medium-high heat. Beat the eggs in a bowl until evenly blended, but don't add salt or pepper. When you can feel a good heat rising, add the remaining tablespoon olive oil to the pan and swirl around, then drop in the diced butter and let it melt and foam.

When the butter is foaming, pour in the eggs. Take a fork (ideally metal if your pan will take it, otherwise a wooden or heatproof plastic one) and stir the egg mixture around in the pan. When the mixture is two-thirds set, stop stirring with the fork. Pinch the chèvre into pieces and scatter these and the spinach leaves over the surface of the omelet. Season lightly (you won't need much salt because of the cheese). Sprinkle with the Parmesan.

Now place the omelet pan under the broiler until the top is lightly set and the cheese is golden. Remove from the heat and loosen the edges with a metal spatula. Slide the omelet out of the pan and serve, cut into wedges.

VARIATIONS

Try one of the following alternative toppings:

Caramelized onion and anchovy Cook 2 to 3 sliced red onions slowly in olive oil with a light sprinkling of sugar until softened and caramelized. Cool slightly, then scatter them over the half-set omelet and top with 4 to 6 snipped anchovy fillets. Finish as above.

Confit of cherry tomatoes Slow-roast cherry tomatoes in olive oil with thyme and seasoning until tender. Scatter them over the half-set omelet along with some torn basil. Finish as above.

Omelet Arnold Bennet Top the half-set omelet with flaked, poached smoked haddock (finnan haddie), creamy Mornay cheese sauce, and shredded cheese. Gratiné under the broiler as above.

CHEF'S TIP *When ready to serve, unmold the parfaits directly onto serving plates. If using metal rings, briefly wipe a hot cloth around them to loosen the parfaits, then lift off the rings. If using ramekins, simply lift out the wrapped parfaits and peel away the plastic wrap. Quickly top each parfait with a scoop of ice cream and finish with chocolate shavings. Serve immediately.*

chocolate and tiramisu parfait

THESE DECADENT PARFAITS COMPRISE THREE LAYERS: *a chocolate-hazelnut base, a sabayon flavored with fortified wines, and a scoop of vanilla or white chocolate ice cream on top. Use a homemade ice cream (pages 158–9), or buy a good-quality luxury brand. To mold the parfaits, use metal cutters if possible (available from good kitchenware stores), or ramekins. As sabayon never freezes solid, the parfaits must be served promptly.* SERVES 6

For the chocolate base, put the chocolate, hazelnuts, confectioners' sugar, cream, and rum into a heatproof bowl. Set over a pan of gently simmering water until the chocolate has melted, stirring occasionally. Remove and stir well until smooth and creamy. Let cool to room temperature.

Meanwhile, set six 2½-inch (6-cm) metal ring cutters on a tray lined with plastic wrap. Or, line 6 ramekins with plastic wrap, pressing it well into the sides and bottom for a snug fit, and allowing plenty to hang over the sides.

Give the chocolate mixture a stir, then spoon into the ring cutters or ramekins. Tap on a surface to level the mixture, then put in the freezer.

Now make the sabayon: Put the egg yolks, sugar, Madeira, and Marsala into a large heatproof bowl. Set this over a pan of gently simmering water and whisk, using a hand-held electric mixer or balloon whisk, for at least 10 minutes until you have a pale golden, light, stable foam, the consistency of thick cream. The mixture should leave a trail on the surface as the beaters are lifted out.

Remove from the heat and continue whisking for 5 minutes or so, until cool. Take the ring cutters or ramekins from the freezer and spoon the sabayon on top of the chocolate layer. Return to the freezer and freeze until firm.

Unmold the parfaits and top with ice cream and chocolate shavings to serve.

Chocolate-hazelnut base:

4 oz (100 g) good-quality milk
  chocolate (such as Valrhona's Jivara),
  about 30% cocoa solids

¼ cup (30 g) chopped, toasted
  hazelnuts

1 tablespoon confectioners' sugar

½ cup (100 ml) heavy cream

1 tablespoon rum

Sabayon:

5 large egg yolks

½ cup (100 g) sugar

1½ tablespoons Madeira or medium
  dry sherry

1½ tablespoons Marsala

For serving:

6 small scoops White Chocolate Ice
  Cream (page 159) or Classic Vanilla
  Ice Cream (page 158)

dark chocolate shavings

CHOCOLATE SHAVINGS *The easiest way to shape thin chocolate curls is to shave them directly from a block of chocolate, using a swivel vegetable peeler or sharp knife. The chocolate must be at room temperature, not chilled in the refrigerator.*

baked cheesecake with strawberries

I ADORE THE CREAMY TEXTURE OF A BAKED CHEESECAKE *and I'm always experimenting with different flavors. Here I have topped my classic cheesecake with a strawberry purée scented with lemon balm. The combination is irresistible.* SERVES 8–10

Base:

2 cups (400 g) Graham crackers
  (1 packet)
⅓ cup (65 g) sugar
8 tablespoons (1 stick) unsalted butter

Filling:

1 lb (500 g) cream cheese
½ pint (300 ml) heavy cream
½ pint (300 ml) sour cream
1 cup (200 g) sugar
3 large eggs, beaten
juice of 1 lemon
2 teaspoons vanilla extract

Topping:

2 cups (200 g) strawberries
½ cup (100 g) sugar
4–6 lemon balm leaves

ALTERNATIVE TOPPING

To vary this topping, in the restaurant we sometimes top this classic cheesecake with caramel rather than a soft fruit purée. To make the caramel topping, place 3 to 4 tablespoons sugar in a heavy-bottomed pan and add a little cold water to cover. Place over a low heat and stir until dissolved, then increase the heat. Bring to a boil and boil the sugar syrup until golden brown in color. Remove from the heat and allow the caramel to cool for 1 minute, then pour over the top of the baked cheesecake. The caramel sets to give a wonderful crisp topping. For contrast, serve a pile of fresh strawberries or raspberries alongside.

For the base, crush the crackers in a food processor, then add the sugar and whiz for a few seconds to mix. Melt the butter in a small pan, pour onto the crumb mixture and process for 30 seconds. Scatter the mixture over the base of a 10-inch (25-cm) springform cake pan, spreading it evenly and pressing down with the back of a spoon.

Preheat the oven to 375°F (190°C). Rinse out the processor bowl. To make the filling, place the cream cheese, cream, sour cream, sugar, eggs, lemon juice, and vanilla extract in the bowl. Process until the mixture is smooth. Pour the filling over the biscuit base.

Bake for 40 minutes, then switch off the oven and leave the cheesecake inside to cool for 1 hour—don't open the door. When cool, take the cheesecake out of the oven, cover and chill overnight.

To prepare the topping, put the strawberries into the clean processor bowl or a blender with the sugar and lemon balm, and whiz to a purée. Strain through a fine sieve into a bowl and discard the residue.

To unmold, run a sharp knife around the edge of the cheesecake, then carefully release the spring side and place on a serving plate. Pour over the strawberry purée to serve.

île flottante

THIS IS MY VERSION OF A FAVORITE FRENCH DESSERT, *which cleverly illustrates the versatility of eggs. The yolks go to make an espresso-coffee crème anglaise, while the whites are whisked up to make meringues that are gently poached rather than baked. To serve, the billowy meringues are floated on the coffee custard and drizzled with caramel.* SERVES 4

First make the custard: Put the egg yolks and brown sugar into a heatproof bowl and whisk until thick and creamy. Meanwhile, bring the cream and milk almost to a boil in a heavy-based pan and stir in the coffee. Slowly pour the creamy coffee milk onto the egg mixture, whisking all the time.

Strain through a chinois or fine sieve back into the pan and cook over a low heat, stirring with a wooden spoon, until the custard begins to thicken and thinly coat the back of the spoon, about 2 to 3 minutes. Do not let it boil or the custard will curdle. Cover the surface with damp parchment paper to prevent a skin from forming and let cool. Then pour into a large, shallow bowl, or individual serving bowls, cover with plastic wrap, and chill.

To make the meringues, beat the egg whites with a squeeze of lemon juice in a clean, grease-free bowl, using a hand-held electric mixer or balloon whisk, until they form soft peaks. Beat in the sugar, a spoonful at a time. Once it is all incorporated, continue to beat for 2 minutes longer.

Pour the milk into a large, shallow pan and bring to a simmer. Spoon three or four neat quenelles of meringue into the simmering milk and poach, uncovered, for about 2 minutes. Using a slotted spoon, carefully turn each meringue over and poach for another 2 minutes. Do not cover with a pan lid or the meringues will collapse. When cooked, lift out the meringues with the spoon and float on the coffee custard. Repeat to cook the remaining meringue. Let cool.

For the caramel, mix the sugar, corn syrup, and 2 tablespoons cold water in a heavy-based pan and let stand for 10 minutes. Place the pan over a low heat to dissolve the sugar slowly, stirring once or twice. When the liquid is crystal clear, raise the heat and bubble until the syrup turns to a rich, dark brown caramel (but don't stir, or stop watching). Immediately remove from the heat and carefully drizzle the caramel over the meringues. Let stand for 10 minutes before serving, so the caramel can set to a crunchy topping.

6 large egg yolks
scant ½ cup (90 g) packed light brown sugar
1 cup (250 ml) heavy cream
1 cup (250 ml) whole milk
4 tablespoons brewed espresso coffee or strong instant coffee

Meringue:
2 large egg whites
squeeze of lemon juice
½ cup (100 g) superfine sugar
1¼ cups (300 ml) whole milk

Caramel:
5 tablespoons (60 g) granulated sugar
1 teaspoon light corn syrup

MERINGUE QUENELLES
Dip a soup spoon into a bowl of hot water to warm it slightly, then dry. Dip the spoon sideways into the meringue and curl to take up an oval. Immediately, tip the quenelle out sideways into the simmering milk to poach.

my baked alaskas

INSTEAD OF BAKING IN A VERY HOT OVEN, *which can be unpredictable, I envelop individual Alaskas in Italian meringue and wave a blowtorch over the surface to finish. The effect is stunning and they taste divine. A candy thermometer is useful here, to check the temperature of the sugar syrup for the meringue.* MAKES 6–8

Génoise sponge base:

3½ tablespoons (50 g) butter

4 large eggs

½ cup + 2 tablespoons (125 g) superfine sugar

¾ cup + 2 tablespoons (125 g) all-purpose flour, sifted

Filling:

2 cups (200 g) raspberries, lightly crushed

6 scoops good-quality ice cream (preferably homemade, page 158)

Italian meringue:

scant 1 cup (180 g) superfine sugar

1½ teaspoons light corn syrup

3 extra large egg whites

squeeze of lemon juice

To make the génoise, melt the butter, then cool to room temperature. Preheat the oven to 375°F (190°C). Line a shallow baking pan with parchment paper.

Beat the eggs and sugar in a large, heatproof bowl set over a pan of gently simmering water, using a hand-held electric mixer, until the batter is pale, thick, and creamy. It should leave a trail on its surface as you lift the beaters out. Remove the bowl from the heat and beat for 3 to 5 minutes to cool.

Using a large metal spoon, gently fold in the flour. Drizzle the liquid butter down the side of the bowl and fold this in very gently. Carefully pour onto the prepared pan and gently spread to a ½-inch (1-cm) thickness, making sure the surface is level. (It doesn't matter if the batter doesn't extend to the sides of the pan.) Bake for about 10 minutes, until golden and just firm to the touch. Leave on the pan for 10 minutes, then turn out onto a wire rack and peel off the paper.

To make the Italian meringue, put the sugar, corn syrup, and 3 tablespoons water into a medium, heavy-based saucepan and let stand for 10 minutes, then dissolve over a medium heat, stirring once or twice. When the liquid is clear, increase the heat and boil until the syrup reaches 248°F (120°C) on a candy thermometer.

In the meantime, beat the egg whites with a squeeze of lemon juice in a clean, grease-free bowl, using a hand-held electric mixer or balloon whisk, until they form soft peaks. With the beaters still whirling, slowly pour the hot syrup down the side of the bowl and continue beating on full speed for 10 minutes to a firm, glossy meringue. Set to one side.

Using a 2½- to 2¾-inch (6- to 7-cm) cutter, cut out 12 disks from the baked génoise. Place six on a tray lined with plastic wrap and top with a layer of crushed raspberries.

Now finish one at a time, so the ice cream doesn't melt: Place a neat scoop of ice cream (the same diameter as the disks) on the raspberries, then top with a plain génoise disk. Quickly cover the top and sides with meringue, swirling it attractively. Repeat to finish the rest of the Alaskas, then place, uncovered, in the freezer until ready to serve.

To serve, place each Alaska on a serving plate and wave a cook's blowtorch lightly and quickly over each meringue to color it. This only takes seconds—be careful not to scorch it. Serve at once.

CHEF'S SECRET *Using Italian meringue is the secret here. Because it is made with a boiling syrup, it is effectively cooked, so there's no need to finish the Alaskas in the oven. It is also very stable and will hold up well while you assemble the desserts. Italian meringue doesn't freeze solid, so there's no problem serving the desserts from the freezer.*

sweet potato pie

ON A RECENT VISIT TO THE STATES *I discovered the delights of sweet potato pie. We don't make nearly enough use of this versatile vegetable in the UK—a tuber that lends itself so well to both sweet and savory dishes deserves more attention.*
SERVES 8

1⅓ quantity Pâte Sucrée pie dough (page 185)

2 cups (500 ml) mashed, cooked sweet potatoes, about 2 lb (1 kg) uncooked weight

3 large eggs, plus 1 egg yolk

¼ cup (50 g) sugar

1 tablespoon molasses

2 tablespoons bourbon

1 teaspoon vanilla extract

½ cup (125 ml) sour cream

2 tablespoons lemon juice

½ teaspoon ground ginger

½ teaspoon ground cardamom

Roll out the pie dough and use to line a 9-inch (23-cm) pie plate. Place in the refrigerator to rest for 30 minutes.

Meanwhile, preheat the oven to 400°F (200°C). Prick the bottom of the pie dough with a fork and line with foil, shiny side down. Fill with ceramic beans and bake in the hot oven for 15 minutes. Remove the foil and beans and return to the oven for a further 10 minutes. Set aside to cool. Reduce the oven temperature to 350°F (180°C).

Meanwhile prepare the sweet potato filling. Beat the whole eggs and egg yolk together in a medium bowl. Add all the other ingredients, except the sweet potato, and beat until evenly blended. Finally add the sweet potato and mix until smooth.

Pour the potato mixture into the pie crust and bake for 45 minutes or until the filling is set around the edges but is still soft in the center. Transfer the pie to a wire rack and let cool. Serve cold, cut into wedges.

CHEF'S TIP *It is important to rest the pie dough in the fridge after you have rolled it out, as this helps to "relax" the dough and reduces shrinkage during baking. Cover the pie dough with plastic wrap before chilling, to prevent it from drying out. If you are really short of time, you can use ready prepared pastry but I suggest you roll it out once, then scrunch it up, and re-roll it out as thinly as possible. Again, this helps to reduce shrinkage.*

crème anglaise

A GOOD HOMEMADE CUSTARD SAUCE—*or crème anglaise—tastes superb, and it can be served either warm or chilled. It complements so many desserts, from sophisticated fruit tarts through to homey puddings and pies, and of course it is an integral part of some recipes, including trifles and bavarian creams. Crème anglaise will keep for 2 to 3 days in the refrigerator as long as you cover the surface to prevent a skin from forming. And although it cannot be frozen as it is, you can churn it in an ice cream machine to make wonderful ice cream. You may be surprised by the suggestion of ultrapasteurized milk, but it does make the custard more stable.* MAKES ABOUT 2½ CUPS (600 ML)

Put the milk and cream into a heavy-based saucepan with 1 tablespoon of the sugar (this will help prevent the mixture from boiling over).

Using a balloon whisk, beat the rest of the sugar and egg yolks together in a large, heatproof bowl. Slit the vanilla beans lengthwise, scoop out the tiny seeds with the tip of a knife, and add them to the yolk and sugar mix.

Add the empty vanilla beans to the milk and cream, then slowly bring to a boil. When the liquid starts to creep up the sides of the pan, remove from the heat and gradually pour onto the sugary yolks, beating well.

Strain the mixture back into the pan, then place over a low heat. Stir constantly with a wooden spoon until the custard thickens slightly—enough to thinly coat the back of the spoon. If you draw a finger along the back of the spoon, it should leave a clear band. A candy thermometer can be used to check when the custard is cooked sufficiently; the temperature should be 180° to 183°F (82° to 84°C).

Immediately remove the pan from the heat and strain the custard back into the bowl through a fine sieve. Cover and let cool, stirring occasionally to prevent a skin from forming. Chill until required (or churn into ice cream).

1 cup (250 ml) whole milk, preferably ultrapasteurized
1 cup (250 ml) heavy cream
¼ cup (50 g) sugar
6 extra large egg yolks
2 vanilla beans

FLAVORED CRÈME ANGLAISE *You can infuse the creamy milk with other flavorings, omitting the vanilla beans. For a minted crème anglaise, for example, add the leaves from 6 mint sprigs to the hot creamy milk and set aside to infuse for 30 minutes, then remove the leaves and return the milk to a boil before adding to the yolk and sugar mix.*

classic vanilla ice cream

WE ONLY EVER SERVE HOMEMADE ICE CREAM *in our restaurants. There is always a good variety of flavored ice creams in the freezers to complement our desserts, and most of them are based on crème anglaise. Pale yellow and speckled with tiny black vanilla seeds, real vanilla ice cream is far superior to bought ice cream. The secret to success is a smooth texture, and using an ice cream machine is the best way to achieve this. If you don't have one already, then I recommend you invest in a good-quality domestic machine with a built-in freezer motor.* MAKES ABOUT 5 CUPS (1.2 LITERS)

2 cups (500 ml) whole milk, preferably
   ultrapasteurized
2 cups (500 ml) heavy cream
½ cup (100 g) sugar
12 extra large egg yolks
4 vanilla beans

Make the crème anglaise (following the method on page 157). Cool quickly over a bowl of ice water, then chill thoroughly.

Pour the chilled crème anglaise into an ice cream machine and churn until thick enough to scoop. Either serve straight away or transfer to a freezerproof plastic container, seal, and put in the freezer. (If you do not have an ice cream machine, freeze the chilled crème anglaise in a shallow container, beating thoroughly at least three times during freezing.)

To enjoy the ice cream at its best, eat within a week, letting it soften at room temperature for about 10 minutes before scooping. For convenience, you can scoop the soft ice cream into balls and open freeze them on a nonstick tray (or pack into a plastic container if not serving at once). As ice cream readily absorbs the flavors of food stored alongside it, containers must be well sealed.

VARIATIONS

By adding different flavors to the crème anglaise before churning it, you can create a variety of flavored ice creams. These are some of my favorites.

Coffee Prepare 1 shot of espresso coffee, let cool, and add to the crème anglaise before churning.

Cinnamon Replace the vanilla beans with 2 cinnamon sticks and 1 teaspoon ground cinnamon.

Mint Omit the vanilla. Add a large sprig of mint to the hot milk mixture and set aside until cold. Remove the mint, return the milk to a boil, and continue making the crème anglaise as before.

Caramel Before you start making the crème anglaise, gently heat ½ cup (100 g) sugar with 1 tablespoon cold water and 3 tablespoons (40 g) butter in a heavy-based pan, stirring until dissolved. Increase the heat and cook until the liquid turns golden brown. Immediately remove from the heat and whisk in the milk and cream. Then continue making the crème anglaise as before.

Rum and raisin Warm 6 to 8 tablespoons raisins in 7 tablespoons (100 ml) each dark rum and Stock Syrup (page 164), then remove from the heat and let macerate for 24 hours. Drain and add to the crème anglaise before churning.

VANILLA FANS *These attractive decorations are simply made from "spent" beans. As you scrape the vanilla seeds out (for your crème anglaise, perhaps) make sure you keep one end of the bean intact. Then, using the tip of a very sharp, thin-bladed knife, slit each bean lengthwise as many times as you can, keeping the end intact. Place on a baking sheet lined with parchment paper and spread out the strands. Repeat to make as many vanilla fans as you need, then cover with another sheet of parchment paper and place another baking sheet on top. Bake at 350°F (180°C) for 20 to 25 minutes. When the kitchen fills with the aroma of vanilla, you know they are ready. Remove and cool. Use to decorate ice creams and other desserts.*

white chocolate ice cream

NOT ALL ICE CREAMS HAVE A CRÈME ANGLAISE BASE. *This one is simply a mixture of melted white chocolate, cream, and milk, combined with an inert sugar, liquid glucose, to keep it smooth. We have very fast freezing machines in our kitchens, which keep the mixture churning until it is smooth and firm enough to scoop into balls. At home, I suggest that after churning the mixture in your domestic ice cream machine, you transfer it to a suitable container and leave it in the freezer for an hour or two before scooping into balls. Good quality white chocolate is essential.* MAKES ABOUT 4 CUPS (900 ML)

Break up the chocolate into a large, heatproof bowl and add the remaining ingredients. Set the bowl over a pan of gently simmering water and heat slowly, stirring frequently, until the chocolate melts smoothly into the liquid. Don't let the mixture become too hot or the chocolate might "seize." It should be just warm enough for the chocolate to melt and blend smoothly.

Remove the bowl from the pan and pour the mixture into a cold bowl. Leave until quite cold, then pour into an ice cream machine and churn until it is as thick as possible. Scoop into a freezerproof container and freeze for 2 to 3 hours or until it is firm enough to scoop into balls.

For convenience, you can scoop the ice cream into small balls and open freeze these on a tray lined with a sheet of parchment paper: Freeze until solid, then place in a freezerproof container and keep frozen until ready to serve.

5½ oz (160 g) white chocolate
1 cup (250 ml) heavy cream
2 cups (500 ml) whole milk
7 tablespoons (50 g) confectioners' sugar
7 tablespoons (140 g) liquid glucose or light corn syrup

CHEF'S TIP *The addition of liquid glucose or light corn syrup inhibits crystallization in the ice cream.*

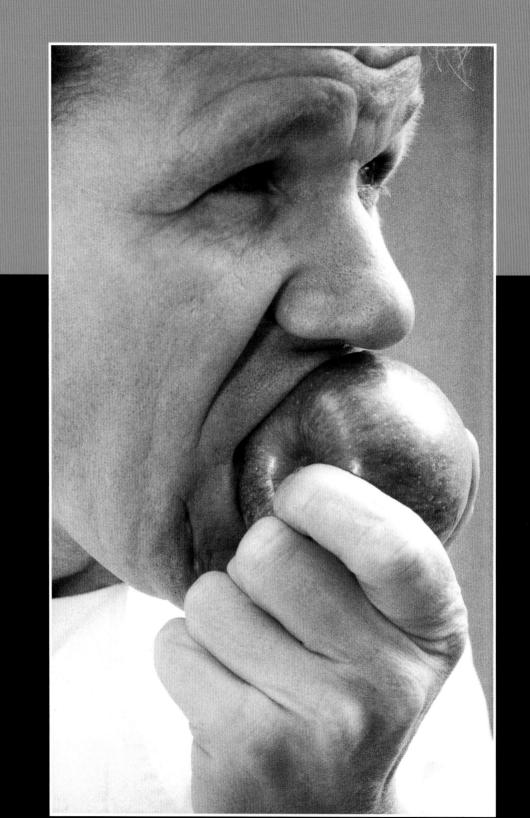

FRUIT

LIKE VEGETABLES, *I love to make the most of seasonal fruits and, similarly, I am influenced by favorites from my childhood. I grew up with traditional country fruits—plums, pears, and apples plucked from trees, and luscious summer berries gathered at every opportunity.*

Semi-wild rhubarb grew in our garden, and I've eaten more rhubarb crumbles than I could possibly remember. If we were hungry before "tea" was ready, we would be given a stick of raw rhubarb and a pot of sugar—the ultimate dipstick. Those happy memories later inspired me to create a roasted rhubarb and custard crème brûlée, which was a huge success at the Aubergine, my first restaurant. It is the satisfaction of taking an everyday ingredient and getting the maximum from it that drives me to be creative.

Desserts have certainly moved forward from my student days. I remember learning how to massacre fresh pineapple, by pulverizing the pulp, mixing it with cassis and lots of whipped cream, and then piling it back into the shell. I have no idea why Pineapple Romanof was the highlight of the dessert cart.

Now I prefer to treat fruit with respect. Plump, ripe plums, pink-blushed apricots, and fragrant Italian peaches deserve to be appreciated in their natural form. You cannot get much simpler than roasted peaches on brioche toast. But if we want to take this dish a stage further, by steeping the peaches in a fresh basil syrup or scattering some crystallized cilantro leaves on them, we can do so without masking the flavors.

knickerbocker glories

THIS IS MY CHIC VERSION *of the favorite British sundae that takes its name from the striped pantaloons worn by Victorian ladies at the seaside. Here, tall glasses are filled with delicate layers of fresh orange gelatin, panna cotta, crushed amaretti, and sliced peaches, then topped with ice cream and a flamboyant fruit finish to serve.* SERVES 4–6

Orange gelatin:

3 cups (700 ml) fresh orange juice

2–3 tablespoons confectioners' sugar

3 sheets leaf gelatin (or 2 teaspoons powdered unflavored gelatin)

Panna cotta:

4 sheets leaf gelatin (or 1 tablespoon powdered unflavored gelatin)

2½ cups (600 ml) heavy cream

⅔ cup (150 ml) milk

¾ cup (150 g) granulated sugar

grated zest of 1 orange

2 tablespoons white rum (optional)

For serving:

3–4 oz (75–100 g) strawberries, finely chopped (about ¾ cup)

6–8 amaretti cookies, crushed

2 ripe peaches, thinly sliced

8–10 small scoops of good-quality vanilla ice cream (preferably homemade, page 158)

dried pineapple and star fruit slices (optional, see below)

For the gelatin, put the orange juice into a pan with the confectioners' sugar to taste and boil to reduce to about 2 cups (500 ml). Meanwhile, soak the gelatin leaves in cold water until softened. (Or, soak powdered gelatin in 2 tablespoons cold water until spongy.)

Remove the gelatin leaves from the cold water and squeeze out excess water, then slide them into the hot orange liquid (or add the softened gelatin) and stir briskly until dissolved. Cool to room temperature. Pour 2 tablespoons into each glass and chill until set. Pour the rest into a shallow bowl and chill until set.

For the panna cotta, soak the gelatin leaves in cold water until floppy. (Or, soak powdered gelatin in 2 tablespoons cold water until spongy.)

Slowly bring the cream and milk to a boil in a large saucepan, stirring. Lower the heat and bubble gently for about 5 minutes to reduce by about one-third. Remove the gelatin leaves from the cold water and squeeze out excess water. Take the pan off the heat. Stir in the sugar and orange zest, then slide in the gelatin (or add the softened gelatin), stirring until dissolved. Cool slightly, then mix in the rum, if using. Transfer to a bowl and set aside to cool.

Pour 2 tablespoons of panna cotta on top of the set orange gelatin in each glass and chill to set. Pour the rest into a shallow bowl and chill until set.

Turn the set orange gelatin out of the shallow bowl onto a sheet of parchment paper and chop finely, using a sharp knife dipped in cold water. Add a thin layer of finely chopped strawberries to each glass, then a layer of chopped gelatin.

Stir the softly set panna cotta in the bowl, then spoon a layer on top of the chopped gelatin. Add crushed amaretti, then arrange the peach slices on top. Finally, as a crowning glory, top the peaches with two scoops of vanilla ice cream and finish with dried fruit slices or sliced strawberries. Serve immediately.

DRIED FRUIT SLICES *Oven-dried, wafer-thin slices of firm fruit, such as pineapple, apple, banana, and star fruit (illustrated right), make a stunning decoration. Simply cut slightly underripe fruit into very fine slices, using a sharp, serrated fruit knife. Sprinkle fruit that is liable to discoloration, such as banana, with lemon juice. Dip the fruit slices quickly into Stock Syrup (page 164) and shake off excess, then lay them on baking sheets lined with silicone cooking mats. Leave in the oven on its lowest setting for at least 2 hours until firm and almost translucent. The slices will crisp up on cooling. Store in airtight plastic containers for up to a week.*

fruit salad with pomegranate

MAKE THE MOST OF TROPICAL FRUITS *during the winter when they are in good supply and other fruits are limited. Put them together in a vibrant fruit salad to brighten the winter days. Pomegranates are in season in October and November, and their fragrant, juicy seeds add a special quality to this salad. Vary the flavor of the stock syrup according to taste. I suggest aromatic angostura bitters and a dash of grenadine syrup to accentuate the pomegranate flavor.* SERVES 6–8

1 cup (250 ml) Stock Syrup (see below)

juice of 2 lemons

1 tablespoon angostura bitters

2–3 tablespoons grenadine syrup

1 medium, ripe pineapple

1 large, ripe mango

1 large peach

1 Asian pear

1 star fruit

2 kiwifruit, peeled

8 oz (225 g) strawberries, hulled

1–2 pomegranates

1 papaya

Mix the syrup with ½ cup (100 ml) boiling water, then stir in the lemon juice, angostura bitters, and grenadine.

Prepare the fruits: Peel the pineapple and remove the "eyes" with the tip of a vegetable peeler or sharp knife. Cut into quarters, remove the core, and cut the flesh into bite-sized chunks. Place in a large bowl and pour on the syrup.

Cut the mango down either side of the large pit. Peel away the skin and cut the flesh into small cubes. Add to the bowl.

Dip the peach briefly into hot water to loosen the skin, then peel. Cut in half, twist to separate, and thinly slice the flesh. Peel, quarter, and core the Asian pear, then slice thinly. Slice the star fruit and kiwifruit. Halve or quarter the strawberries. Add all these fruits to the bowl and stir gently to combine. Chill until ready to serve.

To prepare the pomegranate(s), halve vertically, then carefully scrape out the fleshy seeds. It is important to remove all of the creamy yellow membrane, which is very bitter.

Add the papaya just before serving: Cut in half, scoop out and discard the seeds, and peel, then cut the flesh into small chunks. Gently stir these into the fruit salad. Transfer to a serving bowl and scatter on the pomegranate seeds.

STOCK SYRUP
This has many uses, so I suggest you make up a large quantity of full-strength syrup, using 2 cups (500 ml) water and 2½ cups (500 g) sugar. Dissolve the sugar in the water in a heavy-based pan over a low heat, then bring to a boil and boil for 5 minutes. Cool, then pour into a jar and keep in the refrigerator (for up to 2 weeks) to use as required. For a light stock syrup you will need to dilute it, adding about half the volume of water. Impart character and color by adding flavorings, such as pared strips of citrus zest, mint sprigs, bruised lemon grass stalks, or a dash of liqueur such as Malibu, Amaretto, or Kahlua.

autumn fruits in blackberry syrup

EARLY AUTUMN IS THE TIME *to feature flavorful, ripe orchard and hedgerow fruits in desserts. For a simple compote, pan-roast apples and pears until lightly caramelized, then macerate in syrup with poire eau-de-vie or Calvados and some crushed blackberries. Serve chilled, with cream.* SERVES 4–6

Quarter, core, and slice the apples and pears, but don't peel them. Heat a large, heavy-based, nonstick frying pan until you can see a faint haze rising.

Toss the sliced fruits in the confectioners' sugar, then immediately tip them into the frying pan and spread out in a single layer. Leave for about 20 seconds until the undersides are beginning to caramelize, then turn each piece to lightly color the other sides. You only need to caramelize the outside—the fruit should still remain firm. Tip the hot fruits into a bowl.

Lightly crush the berries in a bowl, using a fork, and pour in the syrup. Add the poire eau-de-vie or Calvados, if using, and toss to mix.

Add the berries and syrup to the caramelized apples and pears and stir gently, then set aside to cool and let the flavors mingle. Cover and chill in the refrigerator until required.

To serve, give the fruits a gentle stir, then sprinkle with chopped mint, if desired. Serve with cream.

2 large, fresh pippin apples

2 large Bosc or Bartlett pears

4 tablespoons confectioners' sugar, sifted

5 oz (150 g) blackberries or elderberries (about 1 heaped cup)

1 cup (250 ml) Stock Syrup (page 164)

2 tablespoons poire eau-de-vie or Calvados (optional)

1 tablespoon chopped mint (optional)

PAN-ROASTING FRUITS
Tossing autumn fruits, such as apples and pears, in confectioners' sugar, then searing them in a very hot, dry pan gives them a fabulous caramelized flavor and color. Brief cooking is essential, as the fruit slices should remain intact.

pear sorbet

THIS REFRESHING SORBET *is an ideal palate-cleanser to serve between courses, or as a light dessert to round off a rich meal. I find the flavor of red-skinned pears is especially good. My favorite is the bright Forelle, which has an amazing flavor, but red Bartlett and Comice pears work well, too.* SERVES 4–6

6 pears, just ripe but still firm

juice of 1 lemon

1 cinnamon stick

4 star anise

1 vanilla bean

1 cup (250 ml) Stock Syrup (page 164)

Peel, quarter, and core the pears, then cut into chunks. Place in a large pan with the lemon juice, cinnamon, and star anise. Slit the vanilla bean lengthwise, scrape out the seeds, and add them to the pan with the empty bean.

Pour the stock syrup over the pears and bring to a boil. Lower the heat and simmer gently for 10 to 15 minutes, or until the pears soften. Remove the whole spices and vanilla bean. Let the pears cool in the liquid, then drain in a strainer set over a bowl to save the stock syrup.

Purée the pears in a blender or food processor, gradually adding the reserved stock syrup. Pour the purée into a bowl, cover, and chill thoroughly, then churn in an ice cream machine to a thick, softly frozen texture. Either serve at once, or transfer to a freezer container, seal, and store in the freezer for up to 2 weeks.

If you are serving the sorbet from the freezer, let it soften slightly at room temperature for 10 minutes. Scoop into balls and serve in small glass dishes, with small, crisp cookies, if desired.

VARIATION

For an apple and pear sorbet, replace 3 pears with Granny Smith apples. The sharpness of the apples complements the mellow sweetness of the pears perfectly.

chilled plum soup

AS A REFRESHING DESSERT TO IMPRESS, *serve this sensational ice-cold soup rather than a sorbet. For an intense, rich color, buy dark-skinned plums at their peak of ripeness. Serve in elegant bowls or wide glasses lined with wafer-thin plum slices. A spiral of creamy yogurt adds a sophisticated finishing touch—no one will guess it's simply squeezed from a plastic bottle. (Illustrated on page 169)* SERVES 4

Halve and pit the plums. Set aside the 6 best halves for serving; cut the rest into quarters. Heat a wide, shallow, heavy-based pan until you can see a faint haze rising.

Toss the plum quarters in the confectioners' sugar, then immediately tip them into the pan and spread out in a single layer, adding the cinnamon, vanilla beans, orange zest, and star anise. Cook, without moving them, for about 20 seconds until beginning to caramelize underneath. Turn to lightly color the other sides.

Mix the stock syrup with ½ cup (100 ml) boiling water and the corn syrup, then pour into the pan. Bring to a boil, then lower the heat and simmer for 10 to 15 minutes until the plums are softened.

Set aside to cool, then remove the cinnamon, vanilla beans, orange zest, and star anise. Tip the plums and syrup into a blender or food processor and whiz to a smooth purée. Rub this through a fine chinois or other sieve into a bowl, using the back of a ladle. Cover the bowl with plastic wrap and chill the soup until required.

When ready to serve, slice the reserved plum halves as thinly as possible and use to line the sides of four shallow dessert glasses or glass bowls. Carefully pour in the soup. Stir the yogurt until smooth and runny, then trickle on top of the soup. Serve immediately.

1 lb (500 g) ripe, dark red plums
3 tablespoons confectioners' sugar, sifted
2 cinnamon sticks
2 vanilla beans (empty beans with the
  seeds scraped out will do)
finely pared strips of zest from
  1 orange
2 star anise
7 fl oz (200 ml) Stock Syrup (page 164)
1 tablespoon light corn syrup
1 cup (200 g) creamy, plain yogurt,
  for serving

CHEF'S TIP *The simplest finishes are often the most effective. To create the effect illustrated in the photograph, put the yogurt into a clean (squeezable) plastic bottle, replace the top, and squeeze a spiral of thin yogurt onto each portion of soup.*

CHEF'S TIP *We always use leaf gelatin because it softens and dissolves more easily than powdered unflavored gelatin, without "clumping." However, you do need to ensure the liquid you are adding the leaves to is very hot (just below boiling point) or the setting quality may be adversely affected.*

melon and grape gelatin

FRUIT GELATINS ARE WONDERFULLY REFRESHING *and always popular with our guests. We serve them in small shot glasses topped with a float of cream or yogurt. I like to experiment with new flavors—melon with grape is one of our recent successes. You need a fruit that is soft enough to purée, for a clean, fresh taste. A fragrant melon that is almost overripe can be used here. Passing the purée through a jelly bag helps to clarify the juice, but it's not vital.* SERVES 4–6

Halve the melon and scoop out the seeds. Using a tiny melon baller, scoop out about 16 balls and set aside.

Scoop the remaining melon flesh from the skin and place in a blender or food processor with the lemon juice. Purée until smooth, then whiz in the stock syrup.

For a clear gelatin, pour the melon purée into a jelly bag suspended from a hook, or a large strainer lined with wet cheesecloth, placed over a bowl. Let the liquid drip through (rather than press it). It may take an hour or so for all the juice to drip through. You should have around 2 cups (500 ml). (If a crystal clear set isn't your goal, just skip this stage.)

Soak the gelatin leaves in cold water to cover until floppy. (Or, soak powdered gelatin in 2 tablespoons cold water until spongy.)

Heat the melon juice until on the point of boiling. Remove the gelatin leaves from the cold water and squeeze out excess. Take the melon juice off the heat and slide in the gelatin (or add the softened gelatin), stirring until dissolved. Set aside to cool.

Meanwhile, peel the grapes, if desired (but not if you're short of time). Pour a little melon gelatin into four to six glasses and add a few melon balls and a few grapes. Chill until set. Add another layer of cool liquid gelatin and fruit. Chill again until set. Repeat the layers, chilling each to set, until you reach the top of the glasses. Chill until ready to serve.

1 well-ripened cantaloupe
1 tablespoon lemon juice
½ cup (100 ml) Stock Syrup (page 164)
3 sheets leaf gelatin (or 2 teaspoons powdered unflavored gelatin)
½ cup (70 g) small seedless grapes

CHEF'S TIP *Setting the fruits within the gelatin in layers ensures they are evenly distributed. If you add them altogether the fruit will settle in a layer on the top of the gelatin.*

walnut cake with italian oranges

THIS DESSERT IS BASED ON ONE OF MY RESTAURANT FAVORITES, *and I love the combination of flavors. A generous slice of warm walnut cake is served with fresh orange segments in a Cointreau-flavored syrup, and a generous scoop of espresso flavored ice cream. Irresistible. In the restaurant, we toast the walnut cake slices under a very hot salamander. At home, you could use a cook's blowtorch to create the same effect.* SERVES 4–6

½ cup (125 g) unsalted butter

¾ cup plus 1 tablespoon (165 g) sugar

¼ cup (25 g) all-purpose flour

⅔ cup (160 ml) egg whites (about
    4 large whites)

1¼ cups (150 g) ground walnuts

Italian oranges:

2 large oranges, preferably Italian

½ cup (125 ml) Stock Syrup (page
    164)

2 tablespoons Cointreau or Triple Sec

To serve:

4–6 scoops good-quality coffee ice
    cream (preferably homemade, page
    158)

Heat the butter in small pan until it starts to turn brown. Strain through a fine sieve into a bowl and let cool, then chill until solid, but still soft. Preheat the oven to 375°F (190°C).

Meanwhile, prepare the oranges. Using a sharp knife, peel away the skin and pith. Then carefully run the knife down the sides of each segment, releasing it from the membrane (working over a bowl to catch the juice). Allow the segments to drop into the bowl. Add the stock syrup and Cointreau, stir gently, and leave for 1 hour.

For the walnut cake, grease a 1 lb (500 g) loaf pan and line with parchment paper. Beat the butter and sugar together, using a hand-held electric whisk or wooden spoon, until light and fluffy. In another clean bowl, whisk the egg whites until holding peaks. Fold half of the whisked egg white into the creamed mixture, then carefully fold in the flour and the rest of the egg whites. Finally fold in the ground walnuts.

Transfer the cake batter to the prepared loaf pan and level the top. Bake for 40 to 50 minutes or until golden brown in color and firm to the touch. To check that the cake is done, insert a metal skewer in the center—it should come out clean. Unmold the cake and place on a wire rack to cool.

To serve, cut the walnut cake into thick slices while it is still warm. Place a slice on each serving plate with a scoop of coffee ice cream and a generous spoonful of oranges alongside.

CHEF'S SECRET *I choose to use Italian oranges for their size and superior taste, but you can use other oranges, or another citrus fruit if you prefer. The sugar syrup and alcohol act as a preservative, so you can prepare the fruit in advance and keep it in the fridge for up to a week.*

caramel bananas with chocolate sauce

IF YOU ENJOY BAKED BANANAS AS A DESSERT, *then this creamy caramel version should please. Bananas are baked in paper pouches along with a rich caramel sauce. Serve the bananas in their pouches for your guests to open at the table, passing around the chocolate sauce in a pitcher. A scoop of pistachio or toasted almond ice cream would be a perfect finishing touch.* SERVES 4

6 just ripe bananas (not too soft)

Caramel sauce:

1¼ cups (300 ml) heavy cream

¾ cup + 2 tablespoons (170 g) firmly packed light brown sugar

4 tablespoons light corn syrup

4½ tablespoons (70 g) unsalted butter

Chocolate sauce:

3 oz (80 g) best-quality bittersweet chocolate

½ cup (120 ml) heavy cream

1–2 tablespoons rum (optional)

Preheat the oven to 350°F (180°C). To make the caramel sauce, pour half the cream into a medium saucepan and add the sugar, corn syrup, and butter. Bring slowly to a boil, stirring until smooth, then simmer for 2 minutes. Remove from the heat and whisk in the remaining cream.

Meanwhile, make the chocolate sauce: Break up the chocolate and place in a heatproof bowl with the cream and rum, if using. Set over a pan of gently simmering water. Leave until melted, stirring once or twice. Remove and stir until smooth, then pour into a cup and set aside to cool.

For the papillotes, tear off four sheets of parchment paper, each measuring 12 inches (30 cm) square. Peel the bananas and split each in half lengthwise. Place three banana halves in the center of each paper square and drizzle on the caramel sauce. Fold one half of the paper over the bananas to enclose them and fold over the edges together to seal.

Place the papillotes on a baking sheet and bake for 8 to 10 minutes, depending on the ripeness of the bananas. To check that they are softened, press the bananas lightly through the papillotes with the back of a fork.

Transfer the papillotes to large serving plates, using a slotted spatula. The bananas will keep warm for at least 10 minutes. Warn guests to be careful of trapped steam as they open up their parcels. Pass around the chocolate sauce to pour onto the bananas.

EN PAPILLOTE *This is simply the French term for baking in paper. The food is sealed in the paper parcel, which puffs up and browns in the heat of the oven, while the food inside cooks in the trapped steam. It is an attractive way to present this dish, although you can simply bake the banana halves and caramel sauce in a foil-covered, shallow baking dish, if you prefer.*

pain perdu with roasted peaches

FRESH, FRAGRANT PEACHES *are quickly pan-roasted, then piled on top of warm French toast for a fast dessert, which can also be served as a brunch. For a limited season, August to September, we get supplies of superb Italian white peaches—for me one of the great treats of the summer. You can, of course, use sweet yellow peaches here, or even nectarines. Top with a dollop of mascarpone or whipped cream and eat the pain perdu with a knife and fork.* SERVES 4

Immerse the peaches in a bowl of boiling hot water for barely 30 seconds, then remove with a slotted spoon and peel away the skins as soon as the fruit is cool enough to handle. Score each peach vertically around the middle to the pit, and twist the halves to separate. Cut the halves into quarters or eighths, depending on size.

Heat half the butter in a heavy-based frying pan and toss in the peaches. Sprinkle with confectioners' sugar and cook over a high heat until nicely caramelized, about 2 to 3 minutes. Remove the fruits to a plate and keep warm. Wipe out the pan.

Pour the beaten eggs into a shallow dish (large enough to take a slice of brioche). Heat half of the remaining butter with 1 tablespoon of oil in the pan until the butter stops foaming.

Quickly dip a brioche slice in the egg and turn to coat the other side, then lift out and add to the pan. Cook over a medium-high heat for 45 seconds or until golden brown, then flip over and cook the other side for about 30 seconds until nicely golden brown. Remove to a warm plate and keep warm. Repeat with the remaining brioche slices, adding more butter and oil to the pan as necessary.

As soon as they are all cooked, place the brioche slices on warm serving plates and spoon the peaches on top. Add a scoop of mascarpone or whipped cream, dust with confectioners' sugar, and serve.

4 large peaches, or 8 smaller ones

7 tablespoons (100 g) butter

3–4 tablespoons confectioners' sugar, plus extra for dusting

2 extra large eggs, beaten

1–2 tablespoons sunflower oil

4 slices brioche loaf

mascarpone or whipped cream, for serving

PAIN PERDU *"Lost bread," as the French name means, has been a favorite way of using up slightly stale bread for centuries. Made with fresh brioche, it is a great base for other pan-roasted fruits, such as plums and caramelized apples, compotes of apricots and pears, and fresh berries, such as blueberries, with a trickle of maple syrup.*

summer berry kebabs

BERRIES AND CREAM ARE THE ULTIMATE SUMMER SENSATION. *Here, flavorful berries are skewered onto dried lavender stalks and served with a lavender-infused cream, for an easy dessert that's perfect for alfresco eating. The luscious, fragrant cream serves as a dip. For more robust skewers, use long, thin, wooden satay sticks instead of the dried lavender stalks. Use any combination of summer fruits—adding cubes of peach, mango, or pineapple, if desired.* SERVES 4

2 tablespoons sugar

4 dried lavender stalks

⅔ cup (150 g) mascarpone

⅔ cup (150 ml) heavy cream

2 teaspoons honey

2 cups (250 g) small strawberries or
wild strawberries (fraises des bois)

1 cup (125 g) raspberries or
loganberries

1 cup (125 g) blueberries

1 cup (125 g) blackberries

⅓ cup (50 g) red currants

⅓ cup (50 g) white currants

For serving:

about 12 long, dried stalks of lavender
or thin, wooden satay sticks

Dissolve the sugar in 4 tablespoons of water in a small pan over a low heat until clear, then add the lavender heads and simmer for 2 minutes. Let cool, then strain the syrup and reserve.

Beat the mascarpone and cream together until softly stiff, then fold in the sugar syrup and honey. Pour into a small bowl and chill.

Hull the strawberries. Skewer together with the other fruits on dried lavender stalks or thin satay sticks. Chill until required.

Place the bowl of cream on a serving plate and arrange the fruit kebabs around it. Sprinkle the cream with a few lavender flowers, if desired.

LAVENDER INFUSIONS
I use lavender flowers to infuse sugar syrups, creamy custards, and even chocolate ganache—the light floral fragrance of lavender subtly enhances sweet flavors to delicious effect. To concentrate the flavor, we use dried rather than fresh flowers. Florists specializing in dried flowers are a good source of supply. Alternatively, pick your own lavender and hang the stems in a warm, dry place to dry out.

FLOUR: BREADS, PASTRIES, AND CAKES

I CONSIDER MYSELF A PRETTY GOOD BAKER. *I love it. Everyone should learn how to bake bread, and do some elementary cakemaking, if only to appreciate the amazing smells that waft from the oven. My mum, Helen, made wonderful cakes. She didn't take a technical approach, she didn't understand the chemistry—to make great cakes you don't need to. Her carrot cake, scones, and lemon cakes were deliciously uncomplicated and I devoured them in no time. Eating and soccer were my two great passions. Mum's approach was wholesome and simple, as all good baking should be.*

Breadmaking, however, does require a basic understanding of how the simple components—flour, yeast, and water—work together. For several months during my early training, I had the responsibility for the night baking at Le Gavroche, and later followed this up with a similar stint in Guy Savoy's Paris kitchen. I'll never forget the night the bread oven broke down at 3am. In panic, I rang the head chef at his home to ask for help... His reply was unrepeatable. The bread oven was repaired first thing in the morning and I had to work like crazy to ensure rolls and bread were ready for the lunch service. The most important lesson for me from those early days was that making bread is like making love—it's a passion, not an item. So no bread machines for me. It's a hands-on job. I like to feel the live dough rising, almost pulsating as I knead and shape, watch and smell. No two loaves ever come out the same. They each have a personality.

pain de mie

THIS GORGEOUS FRENCH BREAD *is a cross between a brioche and a simple white loaf. It is quite to easy to make, especially if you have a mixer with a dough hook. The secret is to make a yeast "sponge" first to get the yeast active. The dough can be baked freeform as a boule, or in a round pan, or shaped into eight rolls. Fresh yeast will give the best texture and flavor, although you can use dry yeast. Pain de Mie is best eaten within a day or two of baking.* MAKES 1 LARGE LOAF

0.6-oz cake (15 g) compressed
    fresh yeast (or quick-rising active dry
    yeast, see below)

½ cup (125 ml) whole milk, warmed
    until tepid (68°F/20°C)

¾ cup (125 g) all-purpose flour,
    preferably organic, unbleached

1¼ cups (160 g) white bread flour,
    preferably organic, unbleached

1 teaspoon crushed Maldon salt, or fine
    sea salt

5 teaspoons (20 g) butter, in pieces

2 teaspoons sugar

4 tablespoons cold milk

semolina, for sprinkling

oil, for brushing

Put the yeast into a medium bowl and whisk in the milk until dissolved. Then beat in the all-purpose flour until quite smooth. Cover with plastic wrap and leave in a warm place (about 82°F/28°C) for about 1 hour to "sponge."

Meanwhile, sift the bread flour and salt into a bowl and rub in the butter, then stir in the sugar. Make a well in the center.

When the "sponged" dough is ready, add to the flour well with the cold milk and mix to a soft dough. Knead vigorously for 5 to 10 minutes, either in a machine with a dough hook, or by hand on a very lightly floured surface. The dough is ready when you can press it and leave a thumbprint.

Place the dough in a bowl, cover with plastic wrap, and leave in a warm spot (about 82°F/28°C) for about 1 hour until doubled in bulk.

Punch down the dough on a clean surface and shape into a large oval. Sprinkle the top with semolina, pressing lightly so it stays in place. Oil a heavy baking sheet and sprinkle liberally with semolina. Place the dough on the baking sheet and let rise until doubled in size, about 45 to 60 minutes. Meanwhile, preheat the oven to 400°F (200°C).

Spray the baking sheet around the risen dough with cold water, then immediately bake for 10 minutes. Reduce the oven to 350°F (180°C) and bake for a further 15 to 20 minutes or until golden brown and crisp on the surface, and the loaf sounds hollow when tapped on the base. Remove and slide onto a wire rack to cool.

PAIN DE MIE ROLLS *Shape the dough into eight balls and roll the tops back and forth a few times to smooth, then press them into a bowl containing some semolina. Place on a baking sheet lined with parchment paper and cover loosely with plastic wrap. Let rise until doubled in size, then bake at 400°F (200°C) for just 12 minutes.*

USING DRY YEAST *If you cannot find compressed fresh yeast, you can substitute active dry yeast. Blend 1½ teaspoons yeast with a little of the tepid milk and 2 tablespoons of the all-purpose flour. Wait for a few minutes until the mixture begins to froth, then mix in the remaining tepid milk and all-purpose flour. Continue as above.*

sun-dried tomato fougasse

FOUGASSE IS THE GREAT PROVENÇAL *rich, flat bread, originally an orange-scented sweet dough, but now more often made with a savory twist. This version, flavored with sun-dried tomatoes and herbs, is my favorite—especially eaten alfresco on a warm summer evening. To give the dough a head start, you need to make a yeast "sponge." (Illustrated on page 182)* MAKES 2

To make the "sponge," place 1 heaped cup (140 g) of the bread flour in a large bowl and mix in 1½ teaspoons of the yeast. Heat ½ cup (120 ml) of the water until tepid (68°F/20°C), add to the flour, and beat for 1 to 2 minutes until smooth. Cover with plastic wrap and leave in a warm place for about 1½ hours.

Heat the remaining water until tepid. Beat into the "sponge" with the rest of the bread flour, the rye flour, salt, remaining yeast, and 1 tablespoon of the olive oil. Turn the dough onto a lightly floured surface and knead firmly for about 5 minutes, until you have a smooth, fairly soft dough.

Transfer to a clean bowl, cover with plastic wrap, and let rise in a warm place (about 82°F/28°C) for 30 minutes or so, until it begins to rise.

Meanwhile, pat the sun-dried tomatoes dry with paper towels, if necessary, and cut into small, bite-sized pieces. Punch down the risen dough on a lightly floured surface. Using a rolling pin, roll out to a 16-inch (40-cm) square. Scatter the tomato pieces and chives or oregano over the dough.

Fold the sides into the middle, then fold the bottom third up to the center and the top third over that, to make a rectangle about 8 by 5 inches (20 by 12 cm). Roll out (or pull and pat) the dough to a square again and fold into a rectangle, then roll out to a square one more time. Divide the dough in half and shape each piece into a log. Keep one covered while you roll out the other to an oval, 10 to 12 inches (25 to 30 cm) long and 4 to 5 inches (10 to 12 cm) wide.

Lift the dough onto a baking sheet lined with parchment paper and slash the top quite deeply at an angle, on either side of the middle, using a sharp knife. Repeat to make another fougasse with the remaining dough. Brush with a little more olive oil and cover loosely with plastic wrap. Leave in a warm place until doubled in size, about 30 minutes. Meanwhile, preheat oven to 425°F (220°C).

Spray the baking sheet around each fougasse with water, then bake for about 15 minutes until browned and crisp, swapping the baking sheets halfway through cooking. Brush the fougasse with the remaining olive oil as they cool.

VARIATION
Instead of sun-dried tomatoes and chives, scatter ⅔ cup (100 g) chopped pitted black or green olives and 1 tablespoon snipped rosemary over the rolled-out dough. Sprinkle with crushed sea salt flakes just before baking.

2⅓ cups (420 g) white bread flour, preferably organic, unbleached

1 envelope quick-rising active dry yeast

1¼ cups (300 ml) bottled still spring water

¾ cup (80 g) rye flour

1½ teaspoons crushed Maldon salt or fine sea salt

6 tablespoons extra virgin olive oil

Filling:

4 oz (125 g) semi-soft sun-dried tomatoes, or a 10-oz (280-g) jar sun-dried tomatoes, drained

4 tablespoons chopped chives, or 1–2 teaspoons dried oregano

puff pastry

HOMEMADE PUFF PASTRY *certainly has a richer flavor than pastry you buy, as well as a wonderful melt-in-the-mouth texture. If a recipe calls for 8 oz (250 g) puff pastry, that is one-fourth of this recipe; for 12 oz (350 g) use one-third; for 1 lb (500 g) use half. Make up a batch and divide into portions, freezing any you don't need to use right away.*
MAKES ABOUT 2¼ LB (1 KG)

3⅓ cups (500 g) all-purpose flour
½ teaspoon fine sea salt
1 lb (500 g) butter
1 teaspoon white wine vinegar
about 1¼ cups (300 ml) ice water

CHEF'S SECRET *Puff pastry rises best when the fat has been incorporated into the flour dough in very fine, even layers. For this reason it is important always to make sure the edges of the dough are as straight as possible when rolling and folding. Simply pat or pull the dough into line. To keep tabs on the number of rollings after each folding, press a fingertip into the corner of the dough to correspond with the number of rollings.*

Set aside ⅓ cup (50 g) of the flour. Sift the rest of the flour with the salt into a bowl and rub in 3½ tablespoons (50 g) of the butter until the mixture looks like fine bread crumbs. (This can be done in a food processor.)

Add the vinegar and trickle in the ice water, mixing with a table knife until the mixture comes together as a smooth dough. You may not need all the water, or you may need a little more. This depends on the flour.

Cut the remaining butter into chunks and mix with the remaining flour. This is best done using an electric mixer. Spoon this mixture onto a large sheet of plastic wrap and shape into a rectangle measuring 5½ by 8 inches (14 by 20 cm). Wrap well in plastic wrap and chill until firm. Wrap and chill the dough at the same time, both for around 20 minutes.

On a lightly floured surface, roll out the dough to a 10- by 14-inch (25- by 35-cm) rectangle—twice the size of the butter. Make sure the edges and corners are straight and neat. This is one of the secrets of success. If necessary, tease the dough into shape.

Place the chilled butter rectangle on the long end of the rolled dough and fold the dough in two to completely enclose the butter. Press the edges of the dough together to seal in the butter.

Roll out the dough in one direction only until it is three times the original length, making sure none of the butter breaks through.

Fold the dough in three, bringing the top third down to the center, then folding the bottom third on top. Give the dough a quarter turn and roll it out again in one direction, lightly dusting with flour as necessary. Fold as before, keeping the edges neat, then wrap in plastic wrap and chill for 20 minutes, or longer in warm weather.

Unwrap with the fold to the same side as before and roll out for a third time. Fold as before, that is, top to center, then bottom over. Finally, divide into portions as instructed in your recipe.

pâte sucrée

THIS IS ONE OF THE STANDARD PASTRIES *we use for tarts. Make up a big batch and divide into three or four portions. Wrap portions you don't need to use immediately in freezer wrap and freeze. For best results, make this pastry in an electric mixer, then knead lightly by hand.* MAKES ABOUT 2¼ LB (1 KG)

Using an electric mixer, beat the butter and sugar together until smooth and creamy, but not fluffy. Split open the vanilla beans, scrape out the seeds, and add these to the mixture.

With the machine running on slow speed, gradually add the eggs. Stop the machine once or twice and scrape down the sides.

Sift the flour and salt together. With the machine on its lowest speed, add the flour in three or four stages. As soon as the mixture comes together as a crumbly dough, turn off the machine.

Gather the dough and place on a lightly floured surface. Briefly knead it with your hands until smooth; don't overwork it. Divide into three or four batches and wrap in plastic wrap. Let rest in the refrigerator for 30 minutes before rolling out, freezing any portions you don't need now for later use.

Before rolling out, knead the dough again very lightly. This helps to prevent it from cracking as you roll it.

½ lb (250 g) butter, softened to room temperature
scant 1 cup (180 g) sugar
3–4 vanilla beans
2 extra large eggs, beaten
3⅓ cups (500 g) all-purpose flour
½ teaspoon fine sea salt

COOK'S TIP *If you divide the pâte sucrée dough into three equal portions, each of these portions will be sufficient to line an 8½- to 9-inch (21- to 23-cm) tart pan. Double wrap in freezer wrap to freeze, and give the dough a light kneading after thawing.*

buckwheat blinis

LARGE, WAFER-THIN CRÊPES *made with buckwheat flour are popular across northern France. For smaller, thicker blinis, the buckwheat batter is fermented with a little yeast to lighten and flavor it, then cooked in small, cast-iron blini pans. If you don't have these pans, cook spoonfuls of batter in a large, heavy-based frying pan, like pancakes. The blinis won't be as neatly rounded, but the flavor and texture will be just as good. Sour cream with caviar is the traditional topping, but blinis make good appetizers with less expensive toppings (see below). Allow two per person.* SERVES 6 AS A FIRST COURSE

Put the tepid milk into a cup, add the fresh yeast, and stir briskly or whisk until dissolved.

Mix the two flours and salt together in a large bowl set on a damp cloth to hold it steady. Make a well in the center and add the egg yolk and half of the yeast mixture. Beat to a thick batter with a whisk, gradually adding the rest of the yeasty milk and the beer.

Cover with plastic wrap and leave in a warm spot for about an hour or until bubbles start to appear and the mixture looks as if it is expanding. Alternatively, for a slow rise, leave the batter in the refrigerator; it will take about 4 hours to start bubbling.

Beat the egg whites in a clean bowl to soft peaks, then beat in the sugar. Beat a spoonful of the egg whites into the blini batter to loosen it, then fold in the remaining whites, using a spatula.

Take one or two cast-iron blini pans about 3¼ inches (8 cm) in diameter. Melt a bit of butter in each pan and heat until you can feel a strong heat rising. Spoon a ladleful of batter into each pan and cook for 1 to 1½ minutes until the surface is covered with tiny bubbles and no longer looks wet, and the sides look cooked. Loosen the edges with a metal spatula and check that the underside is brown, then flip over and cook for a minute on the other side.

Stack the blinis in a folded clean towel to keep them warm while you cook the rest; you should have enough batter to make 12 blinis. Serve warm, with your preferred toppings (see below).

½ cup (100 ml) milk, heated to tepid

0.6-oz cake (15 g) compressed fresh yeast (or quick-rising active dry yeast, see below)

7 tablespoons (55 g) bread flour

½ heaped cup (45 g) buckwheat flour

½ teaspoon fine sea salt

1 large egg yolk

2 tablespoons beer

2 large egg whites

2 teaspoons sugar

butter, for frying

USING DRY YEAST
If compressed fresh yeast isn't available, use 2 teaspoons quick-rising active dry yeast. Simply mix the yeast with the two flours and salt, then beat in the tepid milk along with the egg yolk and beer.

TOPPINGS *Serve blinis warm, topped with a dollop of thick sour cream or crème fraîche and smoked salmon scrunched into rosettes, or folded prosciutto. Or, top with lemon mayonnaise and flaked broiled salmon. The shallot and porcini topping (from Caramelized Mushroom Tarts, page 188) is an ideal vegetarian option.*

caramelized mushroom tarts

WAFER-THIN PUFF PASTRY DISKS *are covered with a layer of creamy onion purée, then topped with caramelized mushrooms and Parmesan shavings. This recipe is suitable for vegetarians if you omit the bacon and use white wine rather than chicken stock.* SERVES 4 AS A FIRST COURSE OR LIGHT MEAL

12 oz (350 g) Puff Pastry (page 184)

3½ tablespoons (50 g) butter

2 tablespoons olive oil

1 large, mild onion, thinly sliced

¼ cup (25 g) diced bacon or pancetta (optional)

3 tablespoons chicken stock or white wine

2 tablespoons heavy cream

8 oz (250 g) fresh porcini or other flavorful mushrooms (see below), cleaned and thinly sliced

2 shallots, minced

1 thyme sprig

sea salt and freshly ground black pepper

1 oz (25 g) Parmesan cheese, pared into shavings, for serving

Roll out the pastry on a lightly floured surface to ⅛-inch (3-mm) thickness and cut out four 5-inch (12-cm) disks, using a small saucer as a guide. Prick the pastry disks and place on a heavy, nonstick baking sheet. Let rest in the refrigerator while you heat the oven to 400°F (200°C).

Meanwhile, make the onion purée: Heat half the butter with 1 tablespoon olive oil in a saucepan. Add the onion, with the bacon or pancetta, if using, and sauté gently for up to 15 minutes until softened but not colored, stirring often. Remove the bacon pieces. Stir in the stock or wine and cream. Season and cook for another few minutes until reduced right down. Transfer to a blender or food processor and whiz until smooth and creamy. Set aside.

Cover the pastry disks with parchment paper and place another flat, heavy baking sheet on top. Bake for 12 minutes, then remove the top baking sheet and parchment. Return the pastry disks to the oven and bake for up to 3 minutes until golden brown and crisp. Remove and carefully transfer to a wire rack.

Heat the remaining butter and olive oil in a sauté pan, then add the sliced mushrooms and sauté until nicely caramelized, about 5 minutes. Add the shallots, along with the leaves from the thyme sprig and seasoning. Cook for a further 2 to 3 minutes, then remove from the heat.

Lightly warm the onion purée and pastry disks. Spread the onion purée thickly over the pastry and arrange the caramelized mushrooms on top. Scatter on the Parmesan shavings and serve warm.

VARIATION

If you can't buy fresh porcini, or simply for a cheaper option, use thinly sliced portobello mushrooms and enhance the flavor with ⅓ oz (10 g) dried porcini. Soak the dried mushrooms in hot water for 10 minutes, then drain, chop, and fry with the fresh mushrooms. The soaking liquid can be strained and used instead of the stock or wine.

CHEF'S SECRET *I love the light crispness of puff pastry but not all those deep puffy layers. To obtain wafer-thin, flat pastry bases, I bake puff pastry disks between two heavy baking sheets. This impedes rising and produces melt-in-the-mouth, crisp pastry—the perfect foil for a caramelized porcini topping.*

blueberry muffins

ON SATURDAY AFTERNOONS, *my wife Tana, and I often take "the zoo" (my affectionate collective term for our four beautiful children) out to tea at our local pâtisserie. Every time I opt for the blueberry muffins. They are a classic example of great American baking and I find them irresistible.* MAKES 12

4 tablespoons (55 g) unsalted butter,
   plus extra for greasing
2 cups (250 g) all-purpose flour
1 tablespoon baking powder
½ teaspoon salt
1 large egg
1 cup (200 g) sugar
1¼ cups (310 ml) sour cream
1½ cups (175 g) fresh blueberries

Preheat the oven to 350°F (180°C). Melt the butter in a small pan, strain through a fine sieve, and allow to cool, then chill until solid but still soft. Grease a standard 12-hole muffin pan or line with paper muffin cases.

Sift the flour, baking powder, and salt together into a medium bowl. In another bowl, whisk the egg and sugar together until well blended, then gradually whisk in the cooled, melted butter. Finally incorporate the sour cream in two additions.

Add the blueberries to the dry ingredients, and toss well to ensure that they are covered in the flour. Make a well in the center and add the sour cream mixture. Stir lightly with a spatula to combine the two mixtures, but do not overmix—there should still be some small spots of flour.

Spoon the batter into the prepared muffin pan, dividing it equally. Bake for 25 to 30 minutes or until light golden brown in color and just cooked (see below).

Turn the muffins out onto wire rack and leave to cool for about 5 minutes. Serve warm.

CHEF'S TIP *I love the new flexible muffin pans, which I have recently started to use. The beauty is that you no longer need to use paper cases or to grease the muffin pan before adding the mixture. The muffins turn out easily and perfectly every time. To test that they are ready, insert a toothpick into the center of a muffin—it should come away cleanly.*

espresso chocolate brownies

I CANNOT RESIST A REALLY GOOD CHOCOLATE BROWNIE, *one that has that soft, slightly chewy texture in the middle, yet crisp surface. Here the coffee offsets the sweetness of the brownie to perfection. Quick and easy, this is a great recipe to make with the kids at the weekend. Freeze any that you are unlikely to eat straight away.* MAKES 25–30

Preheat the oven to 350°F (180°C). Grease and line an 8-inch (20-cm) square baking pan.

Melt the chocolate in a small heatproof bowl set over a pan of hot water, then add the butter and cocoa and allow to melt and blend into the chocolate. Remove from the heat and let cool slightly.

In another bowl, whisk the eggs and sugar together until well blended, then add the coffee and salt. Pour in the chocolate mixture and fold in until evenly combined. Finally fold in the flour.

Pour the mixture into the prepared baking pan. Bake for 30 to 40 minutes or until set to the center but still slightly soft underneath—don't overcook or the texture will be spoilt. Leave the cake to cool in the pan for 1 to 2 hours.

Turn the brownie out and trim the edges if necessary. Cut into 1½-inch (4-cm) squares and serve slightly warm or cold, as you prefer.

7 oz (200 g) good-quality semisweet chocolate

½ cup or 1 stick (125 g) unsalted butter, plus extra for greasing

3 tablespoons unsweetened cocoa powder

3 large eggs

1¼ cups (250 g) sugar

2 teaspoons strong espresso coffee, cooled

½ teaspoon salt

1 cup (125 g) all-purpose flour, sifted

CHEF'S TIP *The quality of ingredients is the key to success here. You need to use a really good, strong espresso—a well-roasted Arabica bean is ideal. Look for a good-quality semisweet chocolate with a minimum of 60% cocoa solids.*

hazelnut sablés

THIN, LIGHT, CRISP COOKIES *like these have many applications in our desserts. We sit crème brûlées on them and use them to accompany ice creams, roasted fruits, and fruit compotes. They will keep crisp for up to a week in an airtight tin, or you can freeze them and remove a few at a time as you need them—that is, of course, if you can resist nibbling your way through the entire batch, as they are seriously more-ish.* MAKES 20–24

7 tablespoons (100 g) unsalted butter, softened

6 tablespoons (45 g) confectioners' sugar, sifted

½ teaspoon fine sea salt

¼ cup (25 g) chopped toasted hazelnuts

¾ cup + 2 tablespoons (125 g) all-purpose flour

In a bowl, beat together the butter, confectioners' sugar, and salt until light and fluffy. Stir in the nuts and flour, and mix to a smooth, soft dough, kneading gently with your hands. Wrap in plastic wrap and chill for about 30 minutes. Meanwhile, preheat the oven to 350°F (180°C).

Tear off two sheets of parchment paper, each the size of a heavy baking sheet. Place the dough between the parchment sheets and roll out to a ½-inch (1-cm) thickness. Holding the edges of the paper, lift onto the baking sheet and place a second heavy baking sheet on top, so that the dough is between both parchment and baking sheets.

Bake for 5 minutes, then remove to a heatproof surface and lift off the top baking sheet. With the top sheet of parchment still in place, roll out the half-baked dough as thinly as you can, then remove the parchment. Return to the oven and bake for 5 minutes or until pale golden.

Remove from the oven and, using a 5- to 5½-inch (5- to 6-cm) cutter, immediately cut out as many rounds as you can while the dough is still soft. Using a metal spatula, lift these onto a wire rack to cool and crisp. If the dough starts to harden before you finish cutting, return to the oven for a minute or so to soften. When cool, store the cookies in an airtight tin.

NOTE To toast nuts, place them in a hot, dry frying pan over a medium heat for 3 to 4 minutes, shaking the pan to ensure they color evenly.

CHEF'S SECRET *Rolling the half-baked dough for a second time between layers of parchment paper, halfway through baking, and cutting out the dough after (rather than before) baking is the secret to these ultra-crisp cookies.*

banana and rum tatins

THIS IS ONE OF THE RECIPES *that earned my Head Chef at Claridges, Mark Sargeant (or Sarge, as he is better known), the Chef of the Year 2002 award. Serve with cream, crème fraîche, or vanilla ice cream. (Illustrated on page 195)* SERVES 4

Have ready a large, cast-iron frying pan (suitable for use in the oven) or a jelly roll pan. Put the sugar into a heavy-based saucepan and heat very gently until it melts. (You may find it easier if you first moisten the sugar with 2 tablespoons cold water.)

Add the butter and melt over a medium heat, shaking the pan to blend the butter with the sugar. Boil to a medium-dark-brown caramel; do not let it burn. Immediately remove from the heat and stir in the rum (it will splutter).

Pour the caramel into the cast-iron pan or jelly roll pan and spread with the back of a spoon to level and cover an area that will take the 4 banana halves; it doesn't need to reach the sides. Let cool until set.

If using fresh "virgin" pastry, roll out on a lightly floured surface to a ⅛-inch (3-mm) thickness, then scrunch into a ball and knead lightly until smooth. Roll out again, this time more thinly than before.

Peel each banana, slice in half lengthwise, and place rounded-side down on the pastry. Cut the pastry around the bananas, leaving a ½-inch (1-cm) border clear all around, to make half-moon shapes. Transfer the bananas to a board, cut-side down, and drape the pastry crescents over them. Press the pastry to the sides of the bananas and trim away any excess, then place cut-side down on the set caramel. Let rest in the refrigerator for at least 30 minutes. Preheat the oven to 400°F (200°C).

When ready to serve, place the pan on a heavy baking sheet and bake for about 12 to 15 minutes until the pastry is light golden brown and crisp. Let stand for a minute or so, then slide a metal spatula under each banana and carefully lift and flip over onto a warmed plate. Trickle the caramelized pan juices over the bananas and top with a vanilla fan. Add a scoop of ice cream placed on a dried banana slice for optimum effect, or accompany with cream or crème fraîche. Dust lightly with confectioners' sugar if using, then serve.

6½ tablespoons (80 g) granulated sugar

5½ tablespoons (80 g) butter, in small pieces

2 tablespoons dark rum

10 oz (300 g) Puff Pastry (page 184) or trimmings (see below)

2 large, slightly unripe bananas

For serving:

Vanilla Fans (page 158)

ice cream, cream, or crème fraîche

Dried Banana Slices (page 162, optional)

confectioners' sugar, for dusting (optional)

CHEF'S SECRET *We use a lot of puff pastry and have plenty of trimmings from the first rolling, or "seconds," as we call them. These trimmings are not discarded, but designated for a different role. We gather them together and mold them gently into rectangles, then wrap and chill to rest. These "seconds" cook to light, crisp pastry that doesn't rise too much—perfect for the above tatins and our flat tart bases.*

CHEF'S SECRET *The ingredients for this dessert are simple—the secret lies in the technique. You will need puff pastry that crisps but doesn't rise too much, and the tatins need to be baked just before serving.*

raspberry and cherry pie

THIS PIE HAS ALL THE ENTICING FLAVORS OF SUMMER *and, as you slice it open, the aromas hit you. During baking, the pastry lid acts as a seal, trapping in the fruit juices, which create the steam that keeps the pastry crisp and light. For convenience, you can make the pie dough a day in advance if you like.* SERVES 4–6

Pie dough:

2 cups (250 g) all-purpose flour

½ cup (75 g) chilled vegetable shortening

¼ cup (50 g) unsalted butter

⅓ cup (75–100 ml) ice-cold water (approximately)

Filling:

2 lb (1 kg) pitted cherries

3 x ½ pint baskets (260 g) raspberries

½ cup + 2 tablespoons (125 g) superfine sugar

2 tablespoons all-purpose flour

3 tablespoons lemon juice

1 teaspoon vanilla extract

½ teaspoon ground cinnamon

For glazing:

1 large egg, beaten with 1 tablespoon water

First make the pie dough. Place the flour, shortening, and butter in the bowl of the food processor and whiz for 2 to 3 minutes until the mixture resembles fine bread crumbs. With the motor running, gradually add the water through the funnel until the mixture begins to come together to form a dough. Use as little water as possible, to ensure that the pastry is crisp and short.

Remove the pastry from the processor and wrap in plastic wrap. Place in the refrigerator and let rest for 30 minutes.

Meanwhile, preheat the oven to 400°F (200°C). For the filling, put the fruit into a bowl, sprinkle with the sugar, flour, lemon juice, vanilla and cinnamon, and toss to mix. Let stand at room temperature for 30 minutes.

Place a pie funnel (if you have one) in a 2½-cup (600-ml) pie dish that is about 2½ inches (6 cm) deep. Spoon in the fruit filling.

Roll out the dough on a lightly floured surface until it is large enough to cover the pie dish with a 1½-inch (4 cm) overhang. Using a rolling pin, lift the dough on top of the pie and roughly scrunch the edges to the rim of the pie dish. Brush the dough with the beaten egg.

Place the pie in the hot oven and bake for 15 minutes, then reduce the temperature to 350°F (180°C) and bake for a further 40 minutes. Leave to stand on a wire rack for 15 minutes before serving, with cream if you like.

CHEF'S SECRET *We think little about the role of water in culinary techniques, yet it is the key to so many methods of cooking. When you bake choux pastry, for example, the water in the pastry turns to steam as it boils and this in turn helps the choux to expand and develop its characteristic texture. In this recipe, the steam lifts the pastry away from the fruit so that the pastry remains crisp and short.*

plum and almond tart

THIS FAMILY-SIZE VERSION *of the little plum tarts we feature on our dessert menus is ideal for a Sunday lunch. It is best served freshly baked and warm. As a variation, you could use semidried prunes instead of plums.* SERVES 6–8

Roll out the dough on a lightly floured surface to a ⅛-inch (3-mm) thickness. Use to line a 10-inch (25-cm) tart pan that is at least 1 inch (2.5 cm) deep with a removable base. Press the pastry well into the sides and leave about ½ inch (1 cm) hanging over the rim. Prick the bottom, line with parchment paper or foil, and fill with ceramic beans. Let rest in the refrigerator for 20 minutes.

Preheat the oven to 400°F (200°C). Place the tart pan on a heavy baking sheet and bake "blind" for 15 minutes. Remove the paper or foil and beans and return the tart shell to the oven to bake for 5 more minutes. Using a sharp knife, trim the overhanging pastry until neatly level with the top of the pan. Set aside to cool while you make the filling. Lower the oven to 300°F (150°C).

For the filling, halve the plums and remove the pits, then cut each half into four wedges. Put the butter, ground almonds, sugar, flour, cinnamon, if using, and egg in a food processor and whiz to a smooth, creamy batter. Spoon into the tart shell and level the surface. Nestle the plum wedges into the batter, placing them skin-side up.

Bake for 30 to 35 minutes until risen, firm, and golden brown. Remove from the oven and brush with the jam glaze while still warm. Let cool slightly in the pan, then unmold and slide onto a flat plate. Serve warm, cut into wedges.

VARIATION

Instead of plums, use 6 to 8 French "mi-cuit" Agen prunes for the filling: First soak them in hot Earl Grey tea to cover for about 2 to 3 hours, then drain, pit if necessary, and cut into quarters. Place in a small bowl and sprinkle with 2 to 3 tablespoons Armagnac or Cognac. Let macerate overnight, then drain and use in the same way as the plum wedges.

1 lb (500 g) Pâte Sucrée (page 185)

4 large, ripe, dark red plums

½ cup (125 g) unsalted butter, softened to room temperature

1⅓ cups (125 g) ground almonds

½ cup + 2 tablespoons (125 g) sugar

3 tablespoons all-purpose flour

1 teaspoon ground cinnamon (optional)

1 extra large egg

3–4 tablespoons apricot or plum jam glaze (see below)

JAM GLAZE *This gives a tempting, glossy sheen to a home baked tart. Simply warm about 4 tablespoons apricot or plum jam in a small pan with 1 to 2 tablespoons water and a squeeze of lemon juice until the jam melts. Heat until bubbling, then stir briefly and press through a strainer, rubbing gently with the back of a wooden spoon. We make up a large batch of this glaze and store it in a jar in the refrigerator, ready to use.*

passion fruit and orange tart

THIS TART IS AN ELEGANT VARIATION *of the classic French tarte au citron. For an intensely fruity taste, I first boil the passion fruit and orange juice to reduce and concentrate the flavor. A thin whisper of dark chocolate lines the tart shell, adding a hint of contrasting flavor; it also helps to prevent the creamy passion fruit filling from softening the pastry. Serve cut into wedges, with a scoop of vanilla ice cream, if desired.* SERVES 6–8

Halve the passion fruit, scoop out the pulp into a saucepan, and add the orange juice. Bring to a boil and boil until reduced by half. Strain into a cup, rubbing with the back of a wooden spoon to extract the juice from the passion fruit seeds. You should have around 1 cup (250 ml). Set aside to cool.

Roll out the pastry on a lightly floured surface as thinly as possible, ideally to a ⅛-inch (3-mm) thickness. Lift it on the rolling pin into an 8½-inch (21-cm) tart pan that is about ¾ inch (2 cm) deep with a removable base. Press the pastry well into the sides and leave about ½ inch (1 cm) hanging over the top edge. Don't worry if the pastry cracks as you press it in; simply pinch the dough together to mend the cracks. Prick the bottom, line with parchment paper or foil, and fill with ceramic beans. Let rest in the refrigerator for 20 minutes. Meanwhile, preheat the oven to 400°F (200°C).

Set the tart pan on a baking sheet and bake "blind" for 15 minutes. Remove the paper or foil and beans and return the tart shell to the oven to bake for 5 more minutes, until the shell is pale golden and crisp. Using a sharp knife, carefully trim the overhanging pastry until neatly level with the top of the pan. Set aside to cool. Lower the oven to 300°F (150°C).

Break up the chocolate and melt in a small heatproof bowl set over a pan of simmering water, or in the microwave on medium for about 2 minutes. Let the chocolate cool until tepid, but still runny. Using a pastry brush, spread the chocolate evenly and thinly over the bottom and up the sides of the pastry shell, ideally while the pastry is still slightly warm. Let cool and set.

For the filling, beat the reduced fruit juice, sugar, cream, and eggs together in a bowl until smooth, then strain into a cup. Set the tart pan on a baking sheet and place on the middle shelf of the oven, pulling the shelf out as far as it is safe to do. Pour the filling into the shell until it reaches the top. Carefully push the oven shelf and tart back into the oven and bake for 35 to 40 minutes until the top forms a light crust and appears to be lightly set, although it may still be slightly soft in the center.

Carefully remove the tart from the oven and let it cool. The filling will continue to firm up as it cools. Chill until ready to serve, then unmold and cut into wedges, using a very sharp knife.

6 ripe, wrinkled passion fruits
1½ cups (350 ml) fresh orange juice
12 oz (350 g) Pâte Sucrée (page 185)
1½ oz (40 g) bittersweet chocolate
1¼ cups (250 g) sugar
7 fl oz (200 ml) heavy cream
6 large eggs

CHEF'S SECRET *For a light caramelized finish, dust the chilled tart with a light, even layer of sifted confectioners' sugar, then immediately caramelize by waving a cook's blowtorch over the surface.*

perfect scones

HOMEMADE SCONES ARE SO MUCH BETTER *than mass-produced ones, and I despair that so many people have never tasted them. It takes very little time to mix the dough, pat it out, shape, and bake. I find that baking scones at a lower temperature than is usual ensures that they remain soft on the outside, yet still rise beautifully. Scones are always best eaten fresh and warm from the oven, spilt and buttered—with or without clotted cream and homemade strawberry jam.* MAKES 8–10

1⅔ cups (250 g) self-rising flour

1 teaspoon baking powder

large pinch of fine sea salt

3 tablespoons (45 g) unsalted butter, softened

1 tablespoon sugar, plus extra for dusting

⅓ cup (50 g) golden raisins

1 extra large egg

½ cup (100 ml) ice-cold milk, plus extra for glazing

Preheat the oven to 350°F (180°C). Line a baking sheet with parchment paper.

Sift the flour, baking powder, and salt together into a large bowl. Add the butter in little pieces and rub it in using the tips of your fingers and lifting the flour up high so you aerate it. When the butter is incorporated the mixture should look like fine bread crumbs. Stir in the sugar, then the golden raisins.

In another bowl, beat the egg with the milk. Pour about three-fourths into the flour mixture and quickly mix together with a large table knife, adding extra egg and milk mix as necessary to give a soft but not sticky dough. Do not overmix—the quicker and lighter the mixing, the higher your scones will rise.

Tip the dough onto a lightly floured surface and very gently roll with a rolling pin or pat out with your fingers to a ¾- to 1-inch (2- to 2.5-cm) thickness. Using a 2½-inch (6-cm) cutter, press out as many rounds as you can. Gently reshape and lightly roll the trimmings to cut out a couple more rounds, if you can.

Place the rounds on the lined baking sheet, brush the tops with milk, and sprinkle lightly with extra sugar. Bake for 20 to 25 minutes until risen and golden brown. To check that the scones are done, lightly squeeze the sides of one—they should feel springy. Slide off onto a wire rack and let cool. Eat the scones within an hour or so of baking, while still warm.

VARIATIONS

Omit the golden raisins and add 1 teaspoon ground cinnamon or apple-pie spice to the flour. Or, for savory scones, omit the sugar and golden raisins, and mix in ⅓ cup (50 g) finely grated aged Cheddar or Parmesan cheese and ½ teaspoon English mustard powder. Sprinkle the tops with a little grated cheese before baking.

COOK'S TIP *To save time, simply pat out the dough to a square about 1 inch (2.5 cm) thick, keeping the edges straight, then cut into squares. Alternatively, pat the dough into a round and score it into eight wedges. Bake for about 25 minutes, then cut on cooling.*

devil's food cake

THIS IS THE ULTIMATE WICKED CHOCOLATE CAKE *guaranteed to satisfy any chocolate craving. A moist, rich chocolate cake is covered in a lavish chocolate and vanilla flavored frosting.* SERVES 8–10

1 cup or 2 sticks (250 g) unsalted butter, plus extra for greasing

3 oz or ½ cup (75 g) good-quality bittersweet chocolate in pieces

2¼ cups (375 g) dark brown sugar

3 large eggs

2¼ cups (300 g) flour (preferably cake flour)

½ teaspoon salt

2 teaspoons baking soda

½ cup (125 ml) buttermilk

1 cup (250 ml) boiling water

2 teaspoons vanilla extract

Frosting:

9 oz or 1½ cups (275 g) semisweet chocolate in pieces

½ cup or 1 stick unsalted butter

⅔ cup (150 ml) milk

1 teaspoon vanilla extract

1 cup (155 g) confectioners' sugar

Preheat the oven to 375°F (190°C). Grease two 9-inch cake pans.

Melt the bittersweet chocolate in a small heatproof bowl placed over a pan of hot water, then stir until smooth. Take off the heat and set aside to cool.

Cream the butter and brown sugar together in a bowl until light and fluffy in texture. Gradually beat in the eggs one at a time, then mix in the melted chocolate.

Sift the flour, salt, and baking soda together. Fold one-third into the cake batter, then fold in one-third of the buttermilk. Repeat until you have incorporated all of the flour and buttermilk. Finally, slowly mix in the boiling water together with the vanilla extract.

Divide the batter between the prepared cake pans and bake for 30 minutes or until a skewer or toothpick inserted into the center comes away cleanly.

Meanwhile, prepare the frosting. Melt the semisweet chocolate and butter together in a small heatproof bowl placed over a pan of hot water. Remove from the heat and slowly mix in the milk and vanilla extract. Transfer to a mixing bowl and then whisk in the confectioners' sugar. Continue to beat the mixture until it is smooth—it will be quite runny.

Cover the bowl and place in the refrigerator for 1 hour, whisking the frosting every 15 minutes.

When the cakes are cooked, turn them out and place on a wire rack to cool.

To serve, spoon one-third of the frosting mixture on top of one cake, then place the second cake on top. Cover the top and sides with the frosting, using a spatula to swirl it decoratively.

CHEF'S SECRET *The combination of buttermilk and real chocolate makes this cake both rich and moist. The frosting can be made in advance and kept in a covered bowl in the fridge for up to 3 days.*

dark, rich carrot cake

THIS WONDERFULLY MOIST CAKE *from the Connaught repertoire takes me back to my childhood and memories of my mother's tasty carrot cake. Not only is it easy to make and bake, it is really healthy, being dairy-free and high in fiber, vitamins, and minerals. So, mum, this one's for you!* SERVES 8–10

Preheat the oven to 300°F (150°C). Oil a large loaf pan and line the bottom with parchment paper. Sift the flour, spice, and baking soda together, then tip in the bran from the sifter. Peel and coarsely grate the carrots. Set aside.

Beat scant 1 cup (175 g) of the sugar with the oil and orange zest, using an electric mixer or balloon whisk, until smooth. Beat in the eggs, one by one, until light and creamy. Fold in the sifted flour mixture until smooth, then fold in the grated carrot, golden raisins, coconut, and chopped walnuts.

Transfer the batter to the prepared loaf pan and level the top. Set the pan on a heavy baking sheet and bake for 1 hour and 20 to 25 minutes. Meanwhile, gently heat the orange juice with the remaining sugar and lemon juice in a small saucepan until the sugar has dissolved.

To check that the cake is done, insert a metal skewer—it should come out clean. Also, the top should feel quite firm when pressed. Run a knife around the edges of the cake to loosen it. Prick holes all over the surface with a skewer, then slowly drizzle the orangey syrup all over so it seeps into the holes and around the edges. Leave the cake in the pan until all the syrup is absorbed, then unmold and remove the base paper. Place the cake on a wire rack and let cool completely. Store in an airtight cake tin until required. Serve cut into thick slices.

⅔ cup (150 ml) sunflower oil, plus extra for oiling pan

1⅓ cups (200 g) whole-wheat flour

1 tablespoon apple-pie spice

1 teaspoon baking soda

8 oz (225 g) carrots

1¼ cups (250 g) firmly packed dark brown sugar

finely grated zest of 1 large orange

2 large eggs

⅔ cup (110 g) golden raisins

½ cup (50 g) dried shredded unsweetened coconut

½ cup (50 g) chopped walnuts

juice of ½ large orange

1 tablespoon lemon juice

CHEF'S TIP *Pouring a citrus syrup over this cake as it cools makes it more moist and imparts a tangy flavor. The crust needs to be well punctured with a skewer to enable the syrup to soak in.*

chocolate truffle ravioli

BRIOCHE DOUGH IS HIGHLY VERSATILE. *These little brioche "doughnuts" are filled with a chocolate ganache, which melts in the center and oozes out as you bite into them. Quite divine as a chic dessert or treat with coffee.* MAKES 20–24

Ganache filling:

3 oz (80 g) best-quality bittersweet
  chocolate

3 tablespoons (40 g) unsalted butter

3 tablespoons heavy cream

Brioche dough:

2 teaspoons active dry yeast

⅔ cup (150 ml) tepid milk

2 tablespoons sugar, plus extra
  for dusting

3½ cups (400 g) bread flour

2 teaspoons fine sea salt

3 tablespoons (40 g) unsalted butter

2 large eggs, beaten

vegetable oil, for deep-frying

First, make the ganache: Break up the chocolate and place in a heatproof bowl with the butter and cream. Set over a pan of gently simmering water and stir until melted and smooth. Remove and let cool, then chill until solid.

Using a small melon baller, scoop out 20 to 24 balls of ganache; they don't need to be perfect spheres. Chill until required.

To make the brioche dough, whisk the yeast into the milk with a pinch of sugar and set aside until it starts to froth.

Meanwhile, sift the flour and salt into a large bowl set on a damp cloth to hold it steady. Rub in the butter until the mixture resembles fine bread crumbs, then mix in the remaining sugar. Make a well in the center. Pour in the yeasty milk and all but 2 tablespoons of the beaten egg. Mix to a dough and shape into a ball with your hands.

Knead on a lightly floured surface for about 8 minutes until the dough is smooth and elastic. Place in an oiled large bowl and turn the dough to coat with oil. Cover the bowl with plastic wrap and leave in a warm place until the dough has doubled in size.

Punch down the dough, then knead until smooth. Roll out on a lightly floured surface to about a ⅛-inch (3-mm) thickness. Using a 2-inch (5-cm) cutter, press out 40 to 48 rounds, rerolling if necessary. Shape the ravioli (see below). Let rest in the refrigerator for 15 minutes.

When ready to serve, half-fill a deep saucepan or deep-fat fryer with oil and heat to 350°F (180°C). Have ready a shallow bowl of sugar, and paper towels for draining. Deep-fry the filled dough balls, four to six at a time, for 1½ minutes until golden brown. Drain on paper towels for a minute, then toss in the sugar to coat. Cool slightly, but serve warm so the chocolate center is still soft.

TO SHAPE THE RAVIOLI

Place a chocolate ball in the center of half the rounds. Brush around the edges with the reserved egg, thinned with a little water. Cover with the remaining rounds and mold the dough around the chocolate with your fingers. Press the edges together well to seal. You will now have 20 to 24 little flying saucers!

STOCKS, SAUCES, AND DRESSINGS

I AM FREQUENTLY COMPLEMENTED *on the way I get so much flavor into my dishes, yet manage to keep them light in texture. So, what is my secret? The answer is simple. I start at the beginning of a recipe, adding essences from raw and basic ingredients with stocks, infusions, and sauces.*

Time and heat are good allies. I concentrate flavors by reducing liquids through boiling—what goes up in steam is simply water—the flavor is left behind. To create flavored oils, again, I use heat to extract the flavor from fresh herbs, garlic, or chili, for example. These flavors are readily absorbed and I use the infused oils to enhance vegetables, salad dressings, and so on. You will notice that infusions and reductions feature in many of my dishes.

All stocks are made freshly in my kitchens. Meat stock is prepared with fresh veal, beef, or lamb bones, according to the dish. We use fresh carcasses for chicken stock, and select white fish bones carefully for fish stocks. Using fresh stocks makes a big difference to a sauce or soup, especially if the stock is the main ingredient. You won't need to make it that often. Just make up a good quantity and freeze it in convenient amounts, say 1 cup (250 ml). One point to note is that we do not add salt to stocks in case we overseason them. Seasoning comes later.

Stocks, sauces, and dressings are the essential basic elements in my recipes. If you spend time getting these right, the rest of the dish will follow.

court bouillon

A COURT BOUILLON IS A POACHING LIQUID *used for whole fish, lobster, and crab. It imparts flavor and acidity to give fish and seafood a subtle piquancy. I find it is worth the time to make up a court bouillon for simple poaching because of the added value in terms of flavor.* MAKES ABOUT 8 CUPS (2 LITERS)

2 leeks, roughly chopped

2 carrots, roughly chopped

1 celery stalk, roughly chopped

1 large onion, roughly chopped

2 shallots, roughly chopped

½ fennel bulb, chopped

3 garlic cloves (unpeeled)

1 large sprig each thyme, tarragon, basil, and parsley, tied together

8 cups (2 liters) water

½ teaspoon white peppercorns

1 heaped tablespoon coarse sea salt

1 lemon, sliced

1 star anise

7 fl oz (200 ml) dry white wine

Put all the vegetables and garlic into a large stockpot with the bunch of herbs and cover with the cold water. Bring to a boil. Add the rest of the ingredients, return to a simmer, and cook gently for about 30 minutes.

Strain the court bouillon through a colander lined with wet cheesecloth into a deep bowl. Discard the vegetables and flavorings.

Cool the liquid unless using right away. It can be kept, covered, in the refrigerator for up to 3 days, or frozen.

CHEF'S TIP *Court bouillon can be reused up to three times, as long as it is strained well after each use and chilled or frozen, then brought to a boil before the next use. Don't be tempted to use leftover court bouillon as a stock for soups and sauces because it is too acidic.*

fish stock

FOR A FINE-FLAVORED FISH STOCK *with a light color, choose bones from sole, plus heads. Ask your fishmonger if he has any to spare, even if you are not buying sole at the time, or give him notice to put some aside for you. You will need around 3 lb (1.5 kg). If sole isn't a possibility, you can use the bones of other white fish, but not oily fish like salmon. Fish stock is essential, I would say, for true fish soups or fish veloutés.* MAKES ABOUT 6 CUPS (1.5 LITERS)

Prepare the bones and heads: If using the head of a large fish, remove the eyes and gills, then chop the head in half. Avoid using the skin too, if possible. Rinse away any blood from backbones under cold running water, as this might give the stock a bitter taste. Roughly chop the bones so they will fit into the pan.

Put all the vegetables into a stockpot with the olive oil, then heat until they start to sizzle. Cover with a lid and sweat gently over a low heat for about 15 minutes, shaking the pan occasionally.

Stir in the fish bones and wine and cook until the wine evaporates almost completely. Now pour in the water, and add the herbs, lemon, and peppercorns. Bring to a boil over a medium-high heat.

As the liquid boils gently you will note a scum forming on the surface. This is simply due to fish proteins and is quite harmless. However, we skim it off with a wide skimming spoon so it does not make the stock cloudy.

Turn the heat down and simmer, uncovered, for 20 minutes—no longer or the stock may acquire a bitter taste from the bones. Remove from the heat and leave undisturbed for 10 minutes so the particles settle.

Line a large colander with wet cheesecloth and set over a large bowl or smaller pan. Gently tip the liquid through the cloth. If it helps, remove the larger bones first with a slotted spoon. If you are not using the stock right away, let cool and then chill. If desired, you can boil the strained stock until reduced to about 4 cups (1 liter) to concentrate the flavor.

about 3 lb (1.5 kg) white fish bones
  and heads
1 leek, chopped
1 onion, chopped
1 celery stalk, chopped
½ fennel bulb, chopped
2 garlic cloves (unpeeled)
7 tablespoons (100 ml) light olive oil
  (not extra virgin)
1¼ cups (300 ml) dry white wine
8 cups (2 liters) water
2 sprigs each thyme and parsley,
  tied together
½ lemon, sliced
½ teaspoon white peppercorns

CHEF'S TIP *Make a batch of stock, boil to concentrate, and freeze in two 1-pint (500-ml) containers. Don't forget to label them, or you might mistake this for chicken or vegetable stock. Unsalted stock should keep in the freezer for up to 3 months.*

chicken stock

THIS IS A GOOD MULTIPURPOSE STOCK. *We make chicken stock using fresh chicken carcasses delivered daily to the restaurants, but I appreciate these are not always available to home cooks. Instead, you can use fresh chicken wings. Light chicken stock is used in soups and creamy veloutés, but we also use a dark (or brown) chicken stock for pork, lamb, and game bird dishes. It is made in the same way as light chicken stock except that the carcasses are first roasted in a hot oven. This gives a depth of color and flavor without an over-meaty taste.* MAKES 8 CUPS (2 LITERS)

4½ lb (2 kg) raw chicken carcasses
   or bony chicken pieces (such as wings
   or backs)
8 cups (2 liters) cold water
3 celery stalks, roughly chopped
2 leeks, roughly chopped
2 onions, roughly chopped
2 large carrots, roughly chopped
½ head garlic (unpeeled)
1 large thyme sprig

Put the chicken carcasses into a stockpot, cover with the water, and bring to a boil. Using a slotted spoon, skim off any white scum.

Add the chopped vegetables to the pan along with the garlic and thyme. Return to a boil, then turn down the heat to a gentle simmer and cook, uncovered, for about 3 hours, skimming occasionally if necessary.

Strain the stock through a colander lined with wet cheesecloth into a large bowl. Discard all the debris. If you want a stronger stock, return the liquid to the pan and continue boiling until reduced by half. Let cool, then chill. Use within 3 days, or freeze in 2-cup (500-ml) quantities.

BROWN CHICKEN STOCK *We use this stock to give a sauce some depth of flavor and a light color. Follow the recipe above, but first toss the bones or bony pieces in about ½ cup (100 ml) light olive oil to coat, then place in a roasting pan and roast at 400°F (200°C) for 15 to 20 minutes turning once or twice, until nicely browned. Continue as above.*

vegetable nage

THIS VEGETABLE STOCK IS ONE OF THE SECRETS *of our light, yet full-flavored sauces. It isn't simply made by boiling all the ingredients together. Infusion is the secret. The vegetables are simmered briefly, then fresh herbs are added and the nage is left to infuse for a day before straining. This is the stock we use for our vegetarian dishes and light vegetable soups. Occasionally I combine vegetable nage with some fish or light chicken stock in a sauce.* MAKES ABOUT 6 CUPS (1.5 LITERS)

Put all the vegetables, garlic, lemon, peppercorns, bay leaf, and star anise into a large saucepan or stockpot with the water. Bring to a boil, then lower the heat and simmer for 10 minutes.

Remove the pan from the heat. Push in the bouquet of herbs and stir in the wine. Let cool to allow the vegetables and herbs to infuse the liquid with their delicate flavors.

Spoon the cooled vegetables and flavorings into a large bowl or other suitable container and tip in all of the liquid. Cover and let infuse in the refrigerator for 24 hours or so, then strain through a cheesecloth-lined colander into another bowl. Keep, covered, in the refrigerator for up to 3 days. Alternatively, freeze the nage, dividing it into smaller amounts.

3 onions, roughly chopped

1 leek, roughly chopped

2 celery stalks, roughly chopped

6 carrots, roughly chopped

1 head of garlic, split in half

1 lemon, roughly chopped

½ teaspoon white peppercorns

½ teaspoon pink peppercorns

1 small bay leaf

4 star anise

8 cups (2 liters) cold water

1 sprig each tarragon, basil, cilantro, thyme, parsley, and chervil, tied together

7 fl oz (200 ml) dry white wine

velouté

A GOOD VELOUTÉ REQUIRES FRESH STOCK—*use chicken or fish stock, or vegetable nage, depending on the recipe. This sauce gets its depth of flavor by boiling down the wine, stock, and cream in stages. Occasionally we whisk in ice-cold butter to give the sauce a sheen.* MAKES ABOUT 2 CUPS (500 ML)

2 teaspoons (10 g) butter

3 shallots, minced

7 fl oz (200 ml) dry white wine

7 fl oz (200 ml) Noilly Prat or
   dry vermouth

1¾ cups (400 ml) Fish Stock (page
   209), Chicken Stock (page 210),
   or Vegetable Nage (page 211)

7 fl oz (200 ml) heavy cream

7 fl oz (200 ml) light cream

sea salt and freshly ground white pepper

Heat the butter in a wide saucepan, stir in the shallots, and sauté gently for about 15 minutes until softened but not colored. Deglaze with the wine and vermouth, then boil for about 7 minutes until reduced by half.

Pour in the stock or nage and return to a boil, stirring, then continue to boil until reduced by half.

Now add the two creams. Bring back to a gentle boil and simmer until the sauce has a thin, pourable consistency. Season to taste, then strain the sauce through a fine sieve. It should by now be smooth and glossy.

THYME VELOUTÉ

Use vegetable nage and proceed as above, adding 3 large thyme sprigs with the stock. If desired, strip the leaves from another small thyme sprig and stir these into the sauce just before serving.

LEMON GRASS AND THYME VELOUTÉ

Use vegetable nage and proceed as above, adding 2 crushed lemon grass stalks and 3 large thyme sprigs with the stock.

CHEF'S TIP *You will find that even fresh vegetables, wine, bones, and herbs used to make stocks and sauces have some natural salty flavor and this will be concentrated by boiling and reducing. This is why I always season a sauce at the end.*

red wine sauce

RED WINE SAUCES *are usually associated with red meats, but we also use them for chicken dishes and, surprisingly perhaps, certain full-flavored fish like salmon, monkfish, or turbot. Depending on the intended purpose, you can use either fish stock or light chicken stock as the base—both work well. Freeze any sauce that you don't need now for later use. Resist the temptation to use a cheap red wine; a Cabernet Sauvignon or softer Merlot will give a far better result.* MAKES 1¾ CUPS (400 ML)

First, pour the red wine into a wide, shallow pan and boil down until reduced by three-fourths to a rich, syrupy liquid, about 7 fl oz (200 ml).

Heat the olive oil in another pan and sauté the shallots for 5 minutes until they soften and start to caramelize, then add the five spice powder, peppercorns, thyme, and bay leaf. Cook for another 5 minutes, then deglaze with the sherry vinegar.

Now add the reduced wine and the stock. Bring to a boil and boil rapidly for about 10 to 15 minutes until reduced by half. Carefully skim off any scum or fat from the surface using a ladle.

Slowly pour the hot liquid through a sieve lined with wet cheesecloth. Repeat this process once more to clarify the sauce even further, then season to taste.

750-ml bottle red wine

2 tablespoons olive oil

4 large shallots, sliced

1 teaspoon Chinese five spice powder

12 black peppercorns

1 thyme sprig

1 small bay leaf

1 tablespoon sherry vinegar

3 cups (750 ml) light Chicken Stock (page 210) or Fish Stock (page 209)

sea salt and freshly ground black pepper

pan jus gravy

THIS IS A QUICK SAUCE *using the natural "jus" (or pan juices) from cooked meat, poultry, or fish. The jus is enriched with a glass of wine, but you don't need to open a bottle—a splash of Noilly Prat will do. If you don't have any homemade stock to hand, you can use canned broth (preferably one that is salt-free).*
MAKES ABOUT ¾ CUP (170 ML)

pan "jus" from cooking a steak, piece
  of chicken, or fish fillet
1–2 tablespoons olive oil
1 shallot, minced
1 thyme sprig
1 teaspoon white wine or red wine
  vinegar
1 glass (about ¾ cup/175 ml) red or
  white wine
about ⅔ cup (150 ml) fresh stock,
  or water mixed with 1 teaspoon
  bouillon powder
1 tablespoon crème fraîche or
  heavy cream
sea salt and freshly ground black pepper

Put the roasting pan (or other pan the meat or fish has been cooked in) on the stovetop over a low heat. Add the olive oil, shallot, and thyme, and cook gently, stirring to scrape up the sediment, for about 3 minutes until softened.

Deglaze the pan with the vinegar, then pour in the wine. Bring to a boil and boil until reduced by half.

Now add the stock, return to a boil, and reduce by one-third. Whisk in the crème fraîche or cream and cook for another minute or so. Check the seasoning and strain through a sieve.

classic pesto

WE MAKE FRESH PESTO TO USE AS GARNISH, *often thinning it down with vinaigrette or water and decanting it into a plastic bottle, so we can easily swirl it onto plates of pasta, soups, etc. Purists would use a mortar and pestle, but we make pesto in a blender or food processor. Pine nuts soon turn rancid, so buy fresh ones rather than use a package you found lurking at the back of a cupboard—it's a shame to spoil good olive oil and fresh, fragrant basil.* MAKES ABOUT 1¼ CUPS (300 ML)

Place the pine nuts, garlic, and Parmesan in a food processor and whiz until you have a fine crumbly mixture.

With the motor still running, feed in the basil leaves through the chute, then slowly trickle in the olive oil. Process until you have a smooth purée.

Spoon the pesto into a jar, seal, and store in the refrigerator for up to 1 week. Or, if desired, thin the pesto with 3 to 4 tablespoons cold water or vinaigrette and pour into a plastic bottle with a squirty tip before refrigerating for up to 1 week.

6 tablespoons (50 g) pine nuts
6 tablespoons (50 g) roughly
  chopped garlic
½ cup (50 g) freshly grated
  Parmesan cheese
⅔ cup (30 g) basil leaves
½ cup (120 ml) extra virgin olive oil

CHEF'S TIP *Fresh pesto will keep better if you pour a thin layer of olive oil over the surface before refrigerating. Replenish the oil each time you use some pesto.*

herb oils

I LOVE TO INFUSE OLIVE OIL WITH HERBS *and other flavorings, to trickle over hot vegetables or grilled fish, chicken, and vegetables. Infused oils add instant flavor and richness with little effort. You can also use them in vinaigrette dressings, diluted with an equal quantity of pure olive oil. It is important to heat the oil to at least 195°F (90°C) to destroy any airborne bacteria in herb sprigs and other flavorings, then bottle and seal while hot. This takes 2 to 3 minutes over a medium heat and does not affect the flavor of the oil. It is also a good idea to ensure the bottle is sterilized first, either by putting it through a dishwasher cycle or heating it in a warm oven for 10 minutes. There is no need to use extra virgin olive oil for infusions—pure olive oil will suffice.* MAKES 1 CUP (250 ML)

1 oz (30 g) basil sprigs, including stems
1 cup (250 ml) pure olive oil
   (not extra virgin)

Wash the basil sprigs under cold running water, then pat dry between paper towels or spin in a salad spinner.

Heat the olive oil gently in a medium pan over a moderate heat to about 195°F (90°C); this takes about 3 minutes. Add the basil and stir gently until wilted. Leave on the heat for 1 minute, then remove.

Lift the basil sprigs into a clean, sterilized bottle, pushing them down with a skewer or chopstick. Then carefully pour in the heated oil. Seal immediately and cool. Store in a cool place out of direct sunlight. You can store the oil in the refrigerator, but expect it to go cloudy (this doesn't affect the flavor).

VARIATIONS

Rosemary Wash 3 to 4 sprigs of fresh rosemary, dry, and proceed as above.

Sage Wash a large handful of fresh sage leaves, dry, and proceed as above.

Red bell pepper Remove the core and seeds from a red bell pepper, then slice it. Sauté in 4 tablespoons of the above quantity of olive oil for 2 to 3 minutes until just softened. Then add the remaining oil and heat for another 2 minutes. Continue as above.

Garlic Sauté about 8 peeled, fat garlic cloves in a little of the olive oil to cover for 2 minutes; do not allow to burn. Add the remaining oil and heat for another 2 to 3 minutes. Continue as above.

Chili Infuse 4 to 6 whole, dried, hot chili peppers, according to taste, in the oil as it heats. Or, slice 3 to 4 large, fresh, hot chili peppers and lightly sauté in 3 tablespoons of the olive oil, then add the remaining oil and continue as above. For a milder flavor, remove the seeds from the chilies before slicing. Also try combining the chili with 4 garlic cloves.

vinaigrette

WE USE VINAIGRETTES *to dress a variety of dishes, not just salads. New potatoes, pasta, and couscous, for example, are often tossed in a vinaigrette flavored with chopped fresh herbs while still warm. But I also drizzle vinaigrette dressings over grilled fish and chicken, and even pan-fried liver and steaks, varying the oil and vinegar to suit the particular dish.*

The base should always be a medium flavor, pure or extra virgin olive oil, mixed with a more neutral oil such as peanut or sunflower oil. You can replace part of either oil with a nut oil, but use sparingly—hazelnut and walnut oils can be very aromatic.

I use proportionally less vinegar to oil in my dressings than most classic recipes, simply because too much vinegar can overpower a dish. A quality white wine vinegar is fine, although you might like to experiment with different vinegars (see below). I also add fresh lemon juice for a fruity, citrus hint. Make a good quantity of vinaigrette and store in the refrigerator; shake or whisk before each use. MAKES ABOUT 1 CUP (250 ML)

7 tablespoons (100 ml) extra virgin olive oil

7 tablespoons (100 ml) peanut oil

½ teaspoon Maldon sea salt, crushed

¼ teaspoon freshly ground white or black pepper

1 tablespoon lemon juice, or to taste

2 tablespoons white wine vinegar

Put all the ingredients into a bowl and whisk together until emulsified.

Pour the vinaigrette into a clean bottle or jar and store in the refrigerator. Shake each time you use the dressing.

VARIATIONS

Mustard and honey dressing Add 1 tablespoon coarse grain mustard with 1 teaspoon honey. Or, for a vinaigrette with a subtle mustard flavor, just add ¾ teaspoon Dijon mustard (no honey).

Herb dressing Chopped fresh herbs can be added to the vinaigrette at the last minute before serving—not before, as the bright green color will turn to gray on storage. Add about 1 tablespoon chopped herbs to each 7 tablespoons (100 ml) of dressing. Chopped chervil, chives, and parsley are all excellent in a dressing.

VINEGARS FOR DRESSINGS *To vary the flavor of a vinaigrette, you can replace some or all of the white wine vinegar. Asian rice wine vinegar is milder and slightly sweeter than white wine vinegar. For a fuller flavor with a hint of apple, you could include a little cider vinegar. Aged balsamic vinegar will impart a special character as well as a pungent sweetness. Sherry vinegar is one of my favorites, although it is quite strong, so it should be used sparingly—a teaspoon is enough to lend a mellow note.*

mayonnaise

A FRESHLY MADE MAYONNAISE *is far superior to anything you can buy. It uses egg yolks to stabilize the emulsion and always remains thick and spoonable. If required, you can lighten a thick mayonnaise with vinaigrette, using at least 2 tablespoons mayonnaise to each 1 tablespoon vinaigrette. Note that raw egg yolks are used here.*

Whisking a mayonnaise by hand will give the best result, but you can use a blender or food processor, using 1 whole egg and 1 yolk rather than 2 yolks, and slowly adding the oil through the hole in the lid while the motor is running. The mayonnaise will be paler in color and a little more runny. MAKES ABOUT 1¼ CUPS (300 ML)

Put the egg yolks, wine vinegar, salt, pepper to taste, and mustard into a bowl. Set this on a damp cloth to hold it steady. Using a balloon whisk, beat well until smooth and creamy. Now trickle in a few drops of oil from the tip of a teaspoon, whisking vigorously.

Continue to whisk in the oil, drop by drop at first, then slowly increasing the amount you add to a slow, steady stream, making sure each addition is well incorporated before you add any more. This way you will achieve a thick mayonnaise.

Finally, add 1 to 2 tablespoons cold water to stabilize the emulsion. Taste and adjust the seasoning, if necessary.

VARIATIONS

Garlic mayonnaise Peel 3 or 4 fat garlic cloves and blanch in boiling water for 1 minute or so, then crush and stir into the finished mayonnaise.

Red pepper mayonnaise This is superb with grilled fish, such as red mullet or sea bass. Make up the mayonnaise (as above) and set aside. Put 2 finely diced, large, red bell peppers in a saucepan with 4 to 5 tablespoons olive oil and heat until sizzling. Add 1 thyme sprig and 1 tarragon sprig and cook gently, stirring once or twice, until soft but not browned, about 10 minutes. Remove the herbs and whiz in a blender or food processor until smooth and creamy. Press though a sieve, rubbing with the back of a wooden spoon. Let cool, then stir into the mayonnaise and check the seasoning.

2 large egg yolks
1 teaspoon white wine vinegar
½ teaspoon sea salt
freshly ground white or black pepper
1 teaspoon English mustard powder
1¼ cups (300 ml) peanut oil or light
   olive oil (not extra virgin)

CHEF'S TIP *If your mayonnaise splits, try this remedy: Whisk another egg yolk in a separate bowl with a pinch each of salt, pepper, and mustard, then whisk in the split mixture. It should re-emulsify.*

Index

CREDITS

PUBLISHING DIRECTOR Anne Furniss

ART DIRECTOR Helen Lewis

PROJECT EDITORS Janet Illsley and Norma MacMillan

SENIOR DESIGNER Jim Smith

FOOD STYLIST Mark Sargeant

PROPS STYLIST Jane Campsie

PRODUCTION Beverley Richardson

ACKNOWLEDGMENTS

I am a great believer in teamwork, and certainly no book with this much quality of information and presentation would be possible without it. Mark Sargeant (aka Sarge) is my main secret. He has gathered together the recipes from his Claridges kitchens and cheerfully made them up for the Saturday shoots, where they were beautifully photographed by the gorgeous Georgia Glynn Smith, having been art directed by Helen Lewis. Petite Helen may be, but her talent for design is great and one major reason for the continuing success of my previous books. On the words front I have to give credit to Roz Denny, tester-in-chief and wordsmith; and to Janet Illsley, the project editor, for pulling it all together on paper.

Three other important behind-the-scenes ladies were a major influence for making everything run like clockwork. My adorable wife, Tana, for tolerating our weekly recipe meetings at home and for getting me out of bed for Saturday photo sessions; to Anne Furniss, the Publishing Director of Quadrille, for her inspiration and patience; and finally to my PA, Lynne Brenner, without whom I wouldn't know where to be when.